SEX NOW

Talk Later

Dr Estela V. Welldon

SEX NOW

Talk Later

KARNAC

First published in 2017 by
Karnac Books
118 Finchley Road
London NW3 5HT

British Library Cataloguing in Publication Data

A C.I.P. card for this book is available from the British Library

ISBN: 978-1-78220-521-0

Edited, designed, and produced by Communication Crafts

Printed in Great Britain

www.karnacbooks.com

CONTENTS

SEX NOW

Talk Later

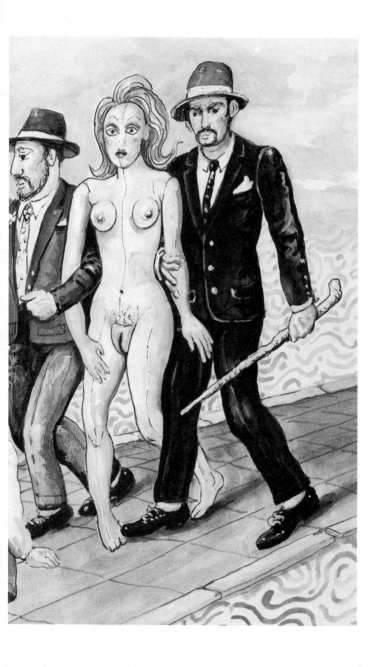

PROLOGUE

The inflatable sex doll

A few decades ago, a young friend of my son (both teen-agers at the time) reluctantly told him that he had received an "inflatable doll" from his parents on his fourteenth birth-day. (It was a long while ago, when these "sex toys" had just appeared and were still made in a rather primitive way, not like the modern robot-like ones.)

He told my son with some diffidence, reluctance, shame, but also alacrity about his discomfort and distress. He wasn't sure how to respond and whether he should be grateful, or appreciative, or even happy to receive it.

I wondered then if he may have chosen whom to confide in, knowing that his confidant's mother was a psychiatrist and psychotherapist.

When my son told me about it, it was my turn to feel rather confused. Were the parents anxious about their son's burgeoning sexuality? Were they worried about his masturbation or even the possibility of his sexual attraction to other boys? Why this bizarre choice of present?

1

This created a turmoil of ideas in my mind, which because of my profession was already busy in trying to understand all sorts of sexual behaviours – or, as others would refer to them, *mis*behaviours. I wondered what conscious or unconscious messages his parents were trying to deliver to this very young man on the cusp of puberty.

Eventually I came to my senses and, harnessing my good will, I began to think this present might have been inspired by good intentions. What if the parents were trying to save this adolescent boy from the potential hurt involved in the pursuit of a romantic relationship, but they couldn't talk about it? What message had they meant to give?

They may have been aware that the adolescent dream of a wonderful, unique, sexually satisfying relationship provokes and produces so many unfortunate, troublesome, and even very sad events. The growing boy could easily feel emotionally crippled by his attempts to achieve that which in everyone's mind and fantasy-life easily emerges from the romantic encounter. It might later advance to a physical realm of the senses where the imagination is spinning and all is perfect – ecstasies of mutually corresponding deep sentiments, and profound and perfect physical union.

This line of thinking led me to consideration of that *real* first relationship, which most of us have had the enormous fortune to experience after birth. Imagine, for a moment, a baby just born into its mother's warm and welcoming embrace. A few moments later, the baby's first experience of hunger, communicated through little noises expressing a need for nurturing, corresponds exactly to the mother experiencing her breasts heavy with milk. This perfect emotional–physical union is bliss! But, sadly, one never to be exactly repeated. As we grow up and try to achieve that quality of relationship, we are bound to go from failure to failure, from one disappointment to the next. Our lives become a terrible chain of increasingly serious failed relationships.

So, I thought that perhaps this young man's parents were trying to help him achieve sexual satisfaction without all the risks encountered in our romantic lives, without the ambitions we have for our relationships when we are still full of the expectations about "making love". Perhaps the meaning of this special gift was: "Okay baby, do not worry too much. Have sex with this doll, practise and enjoy it, but please do not have any romantic expectations. Later on you can go on to try the *real* thing!"

At times our minds are embroiled in the darkness of sex and its meaning, especially those of us already working in psychodynamic psychotherapy with individuals who, of their own will, "admit" and "confess" the "odd" scenarios that can trigger their sexual desires. Sometimes these scenarios are capable of intruding into people's minds to the extent that they are unable to fight against this impulse. These thoughts may appear in anybody's mind, including the minds of those in the mental health professions.

REFLECTIONS

This story reminded me that earlier, during a professional conference in Europe, I saw by chance – and to my extreme surprise and alarm – three colleagues of mine walking along a street with an inflatable doll in their arms. I looked at them in amazement, and their quick retort was: "Well, if they're good for fucking, why not take them out for a walk?" In a way they were able to acknowledge and confound the inherent dehumanisation and objectification of the doll, by treating "her" as if she were a real woman.

So this "easy" approach to sex, without the expectation of talking or not talking, can be found in many people, including our own colleagues.

At another international conference, this time in New York, I was once more quite surprised by the naivety of my colleagues when, at breakfast, they confessed to me that the night before they had been missing their families so much they had decided to see a live sex show to cheer themselves up. To their "surprise", they became even sadder. It had apparently never occurred to them that they had placed themselves in the situation of a child watching the primal scene – the first witnessing of parental sexual intercourse – which inevitably leads to feelings of alienation, loneliness, and rejection.

El niño

El enamo y su novia

ONE

Introduction

Through the course of this book, I will explore with you some situations that apparently go from the sublime to the ridiculous, including the most tragic of circumstances, and which may involve strange scenarios of sexual stimulation and fulfilment in which there is no talking.

My intention is to furnish readers with insight so that when you encounter unusual "sexual" situations, at home, at work, or in art, literature, and opera, you are aware of the many underlying layers. Some of these layers belong to the conscious mind, but more often, for such actions to have occurred, it is the unconscious to which they belong.

We must keep an open mind about the reasons that such sexual situations or practices exist and be aware that often they are completely unrelated to morality. The fact is that encountering – listening to or reading about – unusual sexual activities can easily evoke confusion that, sadly, at times is of such intensity that we respond with anxious or judgemental laughter in an attempt to dissociate ourselves from an experience that can easily be unsettling and stressful.

Some practices that at first are unknown and denigrated are later on accepted, as societal and cultural norms change over time, along with the concept, understanding, and use of pornography, which I shall deal with later on.

For example, I initially thought of the use of a sex doll as a rather bizarre behaviour, but I formed different opinions after considering it less presumptuously. The sex doll is so clearly and cleverly designed that we do not need to "explore" any unconscious motivations to understand it: a man has been given the opportunity to have the "ideal" woman who will accommodate any and all of his sexual desires, who will be always obedient and powerless, and who will never demand her own rights. That is not so difficult to decipher.

So much for men using inflatable dolls. What about the now widely publicised use of sex toys among women from all different socioeconomic, ethnic, and cultural walks of life?

Since the dawn of sexual intercourse, women have learnt to fake orgasms to fulfil their male partners' need to feel happy and like "real men", often leaving themselves unsatisfied. Now they can achieve orgasm using sex toys either alone or during shared sexual encounters, whether with long-time partners or one-night stands.

I think it is important that, as a psychotherapist, I have never been approached by a woman regarding a sex toy problem. In other words, there are no complaints or feelings of embarrassment or shame expressed by either women or their male partners about the use of sex toys. Women and men are explicit sexual collaborators in this respect.

Unusual sexual practices are intensely related to intimacy and have behind them an early, primitive origin that takes us not only to the initial relationship between mother and baby but also to the time in the womb, as I shall try to demonstrate with an illuminating clinical vignette.

AUTO-EROTIC ASPHYXIA

As a young and relatively inexperienced clinician I encountered a most challenging patient with a particular psychopathology I had never heard of or read about before.

> A young, handsome, recently married man came for treatment, not because he wanted it but because he felt he had no option since his wife had insisted on it, otherwise she would leave him.
>
> He told me with a great deal of embarrassment and confusion of his compulsion to repeat, every week, an action through which he derived not only a great orgasm, but which also gave him a great sense of inner peace and self-security. However, this was accompanied by a threatening sense that if anything went wrong he would face death.
>
> His compulsion involved going to the loft in his house where he kept some complicated rubber gear that he would pull over his entire body, including his head, that provided near total sensory deprivation. At this point, uncertain of his own survival, he would reach orgasm.

I met this therapeutic challenge with some fear and trepidation, but I was also very curious to know more. I was acutely aware that my knowledge of the subject was inadequate, and in my search for greater insight, I was daring and not very cautious. I decided on a Saturday morning, while doing my weekly grocery shopping in Soho, to enter a so-called sex shop where I could learn more about the quality of the rubber that my patient found so desirable. To my bewilderment I found out that the rubber, which I had assumed to be of the kind used for underwater sports, was actually as thin as skin. This new knowledge gave me access to meanings and symbolism to which I had been previously blind, and I was overjoyed that my new discovery could be used effectively in the service of a more thorough understanding of the real nature of his problems.

I became aware that my patient, despite his apparent success and well-being, was in need of a "second" skin to be used not only as a protection against all possibilities of pain, but also as a container for anguish and anxiety of paramount proportions.

My patient felt himself to be literally on the cusp of life and death, and he could only continue with his so-called normal life if able to perform this activity at least once a week. So his bizarre acting out allowed him to maintain his appearance of being "normal".

He was aware from early adolescence of his oddity, but he had never confided in anyone about it. He fell in love and assumed, hoped, and wished that he was over his "peculiarity", and so he never "bothered" to tell his future wife about it.

(I shall elaborate the psychodynamic mechanism underpinning this later, in the section entitled "Encapsulation")

The Houdini box: triggering sexual arousal

A few sessions later, my patient told me he had had a very strange experience, which had made him feel extremely embarrassed. The previous night he had been watching television with his wife in the lounge and suddenly and unexpectedly had felt overtaken by the desire to make love to her on the floor, there and then.

In contrast to your fantasies (or mine, for that matter) regarding the imagery on the screen, apparently nothing remotely romantic or typically erotic had been shown. In fact, as my patient explained, it was a documentary on the escapologist Houdini. On the screen was Houdini in a box, going up and down the rapids in Canada, and this had produced in my patient an influx of sexual feelings and a strong erection, which he couldn't control at all.

What was the symbolic meaning of that particular scene?

As soon as I heard this, it brought to mind the circumstances of my own birth and then of his, and I suggested to him that what he'd seen on the TV had represented something very important, crucial to his survival, which extended as far back as to his own birth. He brusquely turned his head away from the couch and said: "I know it was very difficult, though how difficult I am not sure, but I'll check with my mother." Since his mother was alive he was able to talk to her and she told him about the very difficult circumstances of his birth.

Surviving in an incubator

My patient's mother told him that before his birth he had been recognised as a bad breech presentation. The medical team tried to use external manipulation to modify his position, but without success, and he was born three months prematurely, weighing one and a half kilos. There was much uncertainty about his survival, and he was immediately placed in an incubator. Despite being artificially fed he began to lose weight, and he remained in the incubator until the age of six months. It was then thought safe enough for him to be out of the incubator and to be fed by his mother.

This left him in a precarious predicament of which he was obviously intellectually unconscious. He was emotionally extremely fragile and subsequently had recourse only to bizarre scenarios, which were not of his own conscious design. The essential aspects of these bizarre scenarios included, initially, the uncertainty and lack of safety of the womb, offering a precarious, faulty position, and then being subjected to a violent expulsion without any holding space. Only a rigid box, the incubator, could offer a sense of survival.

Unconscious suicidal fantasies

It seems to me now that my patient was repeating something from an archaic time where no language and no conscious or preconscious memories would ever become available. The Houdini box actually re-presented him with his need to grasp hold of life and his virtual "resurrection" even before his own life started as such.

The incubator may have been partly responsible for an illusion of omnipotence, but the price paid for his survival was represented by unconscious suicidal fantasies where he was either evicted (destroyed) or emerged still alive but trapped in a paranoid-schizoid position from which he developed a false sense of autonomy. Over the years this false sense was repeatedly re-created, with its repudiation of intimacy and its false protection. He had become imprisoned in compulsive, repetitive behaviour experienced by him simultaneously as alien and yet strangely familiar and reassuring. Although this was not consciously designed, it was his only strategy for survival.

My dream in the countertransference

If you are wondering how I made the link between Houdini and my patient's birth, I must confess that I owe this insight to my own early psychoanalysis, of which I will relate an illuminating part.

I was subjected to a repetitive, highly anxiety-producing dream.

> In the dream, *I am lying in a suspended hammock with a great sense of space and depth underneath, and I am able to move in a soft and pleasant way. But the movements of the hammock become faster and faster and I no longer feel in control. I look underneath, and to my consternation and great alarm the space is becoming narrower and narrower, so much so that I am really scared since I now notice sharp, cutting surfaces just below me. The hammock shrinks and disappears, and I am left falling into a precipice.* (This is not at all unlike the situation of the Mexican divers in Acapulco who make their living risking their lives by plunging from high up on a cliff into quite shallow water, which requires a great deal of practice, expertise, and courage and an instinct for survival.) I woke up in panic in a cold sweat, relieved to be alive.

When reporting this dream in my psychoanalytic session, I heard my analyst suggesting, in a quiet and confident way, that this was perhaps a birth dream representing a very fast delivery, and that this might account for my own separation anxieties. My mother was no longer alive, but the midwife, a family friend, was, so I asked her whether, by any chance, she remembered assisting at my delivery. Her answer was immediate and devoid of any doubt: "How could I ever forget it. You came up like a champagne cork, so fast and so boisterous,

I had never seen anything like it." So I had "known" about it all along, without really knowing.

I remember later sharing this experience with R. D. Laing, the famous, if controversial, psychotherapist, who had been giving a lecture at the Royal College of Psychiatrists. He himself had spoken about psychic regression to the blastocoel stage in very early foetal life, just after the egg is impregnated.

Collusive countertransference or required knowledge?

Returning to my patient, there were unsuspected problems to be faced on the Friday morning when I presented her case to the rest of the staff in the clinical seminar. In doing so, I explained my sense of inadequacy in understanding my new patient's predicament. Furthermore, I added that my zeal in comprehending it all had taken me to visit a sex shop. This was not kindly taken – indeed, the opposite happened. Suddenly they were up in arms, alarmed about my alleged collusion and "partnership" with my patient's predicament. I felt humiliated and misunderstood. I was immediately overtaken by speculative "interpretations" from my senior colleagues about my countertransference reaction in being "seduced" by my patient. I was infuriated by this and found it very difficult to take.

A response to my senior colleagues' challenge

I was suddenly inspired and presented a challenge back to them. If any of them knew the exact nature of the rubber used to construct the suits my patient wore, I would without hesitation accept their interpretations of my own "acting out". However, if nobody could offer an adequate description of the quality of the rubber, their judgement of the situation had to be reviewed, since my detour in Soho could be considered a scientific one and not an "acting out". This was eventually accepted with some reluctance. To my relief and delight, my colleagues offered a description of the thick rubber used for underwater protection. I was now able to explain what the rubber was really like, and we all were able to participate in a rich exchange of ideas. Anyway, it was a narrow escape. So much for the rough learning about the implications of transference and countertransference in working with these difficult patients.

KEY CONCEPTS

It is through long and comprehensive psychotherapeutic treatment of patients such as this that we have been able to obtain a fuller understanding of the causes of these unusual sexual practices. It is my intention in this book to share with readers the insights we have gained. First, though, it may be worth while to describe some key concepts.

Our psyche – our mind – is inhabited by three different structures, which constantly interact to regulate the expression of our emotions: these are the id, the ego, and the superego, all developing throughout different stages in our lives.

The id is like the small child demanding immediate satisfaction to any wish, expecting pleasure. If this is denied, tension and frustration arise, leading to anger and violence.

The function of the superego is to restrain the id's impulses – especially those that society seeks to control, such as sex and aggression. It strives for perfection. It is a self-critical conscience, reflecting social standards learnt from parents and teachers, and it demands empathy and politeness.

The ego has the invidious task of functioning as a mediator or "referee" of both id and superego and acts according to the "reality principle", working out realistic ways of satisfying the id's demands, often compromising or postponing satisfaction to avoid negative consequences within society.

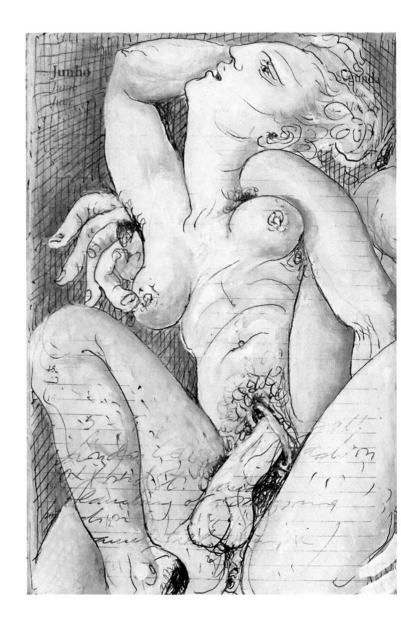

TWO

Sexual release without words

I shall offer several clinical vignettes from both women and men who share a consistent characteristic defined by their "learnt" predisposition to obtain sexual arousal, pleasure, and satisfaction and achieve sexual release without words!

A MALE FLASHER

The following letter is not at all an oddity – in fact, there are many men who are aware from early adolescence of a compulsion to show off their genitals to strange women but have kept their "terrible secret" away from everybody. However, later in life, they experience a need to open up and try to obtain professional help. This hidden behaviour, which so far had been effectively concealed by being extremely careful, now operates in rather clumsy fashion, as clearly explained in the following letter from a male patient, aged thirty-eight, who wrote to me regarding his exhibitionistic behaviour:

"It has always been present, ever since I was thirteen, and has now become a matter of urgent concern. Although, throughout my life, I've been able to conceal this from everyone, including my wife and my close associates at work, I'm now scared of losing everything I have. A wonderful family, my wife, who is a constant support to me, my three children in public school, my prestigious post within the European Community, my friends and associates at work who've no idea what I've been going through. These impossible years have only been made bearable by the fact that all those around me know nothing about this. I am under this strange urge to show my genitals to strange women and expect them to be shocked and scared. When this does happen, I experience a great deal of sexual pleasure. Until now I've always done this in ways that nobody could ever catch me. But suddenly I'm taking a lot of risks. I'm scared of being caught at any minute. I've no idea how to stop it. It just takes me over. Previously I'd been careful and cunning in my flashing, going to places far away from home and work. But now I'm experiencing the need to do it in nearby places, or in a repetitive fashion, either to the same women or in the same places or at the same times. I've found that this risk-taking that is associated with much excitement has now become my only way of relieving myself from increasing sexual anxiety. I'm unable to bear this any longer."

During the assessment period he was able to ascertain his motivation for treatment. Some may say that his "motivation" had to do with trying to avoid a custodial sentence if apprehended. However, in our understanding this is now the equivalent of the neurotic need for the understanding of unwanted symptoms.

Psychotherapy was pursued when he learnt of his sense of impotence and helplessness as a child at being a constant witness of the daily domestic violence perpetuated by his parents. Later, as a grown-up young man, he fell "victim" to doing to others what had been done to him as a child. His feeling of might, and the response of the women "victims" to his actions, were his evidence of his power, which had been absent when he was a child.

TOUCHING THE BREASTS OF STRANGE WOMEN: THE TURN-ON

A man in his mid-thirties spontaneously came to the clinic complaining of intense and irresistible impulses to touch and fondle unknown women's breasts. He had been able to get away with this in busy public places, usually while travelling at peak times on the London Underground. He would stand near the carriage door and furtively stroke the breasts of a strange woman, ready to flee if she started to protest. He had never been detained by police, but felt shame and disgust with himself afterwards, though he was unable to resist the impulses. He was excited at all stages of his actions, including the advance planning, choice of his victim, and then her reaction.

The reason for the request for a consultation was strange, but it was revealing of his silence and the encapsulation of his particular problem, which was known only to himself. A few weeks earlier, he had begun to touch the breast of a woman on a subway train, but had failed to arouse any response from her. He started boldly stroking her breast but was confused when, despite this, she still did not react.

She only became aware of the awkwardness of her situation when noticing other passengers looking at her, some laughing but others shocked. As she finally realised the indignity of the situation, her reaction was to place his hand on her chest and pull out a "falsie": "If this is what you want, you can take it," she quipped and started laughing. The man was overwhelmed by intense shame. He told me, "I had never experienced such humiliation". His immediate association to this experience was to recall that when he was three years old his mother transferred all her attention to his new-born sister and ridiculed him for wanting to continue suckling her breast.

This example is so indicative of the intensity of his hatred of the birth of his sister and his experience of her as his nemesis for the ownership of his most precious possession: his mother's breast. But to understand it, we need to explore other sources of insight. Sometimes "mistakes" can give us strong clues to the content of the unconscious mind.

The replacement baby:
parents' expectations and wishes

The true circumstances around his and his sister's births were uncovered later on, when an incident took place between him and a woman whom he saw in the Clinic's waiting room. He became rather agitated and nasty towards her when, expecting to be called for his session, it was instead she who was called to my consulting room. In fact, he had made a "mistake" about his own appointment time and had arrived an hour early. He had also developed the strong conviction that she was my favourite patient.

This episode gave us the chance to attempt to make some sort of reconstruction of the circumstances surrounding his birth. He had been planned to be a "replacement baby" for the first child, a girl, who had died soon after her birth, leaving her parents in deep bereavement. Sadly and regrettably, as often still happens, they were advised to embark on this replacement pregnancy as soon as possible. This meant that my patient's arrival in the world was met with great disappointment; he was not the expected girl!

Who knows what this small baby had to contend with, but it seems to me that he may have experienced that his survival depended on grabbing his mother's breast as if it were part of himself. With his sister's birth, he may have felt in intense danger and a need to struggle for his survival.

ENCAPSULATION

If we think carefully about all of the above descriptions, there is a feature that is common to each. Nobody apart from the person who suffers from these strange compulsions knows about it. The protagonist has been extremely careful and cautious in not letting anybody know. Why is that, we wonder? Is it about shame, is it about confusion, since the person does not know what is behind the urge to do so? It appears that such people are aware that their actions are painful for other people. If not causing physical discomfort, there is some discharge of hidden hostility. There seems also to be an awareness that their actions are effectively separating them from others (strangers, friends, even their most beloved). In doing this, they preclude any intimacy between themselves and others. Perhaps the protagonists even feel in danger of losing everything if "their secret" is disclosed.

Encapsulation, then, is the concealment of an important part of oneself from others. It is a form of self-imprisonment that combines self-deception and deception to others. The "right arm" knows what the "left arm is doing".

In encapsulation, the protagonist feels trapped, unable to escape his "destiny". He tries to deceive himself and others about his supposed "normality". He courts imprisonment by compulsively getting himself into situations in which he is breaking the law and could be harshly judged and penalised. He convinces himself that he is in control and no longer a passive victim of abuse, as he has unconsciously set up the punishment situation. However, this well-constructed "safety-net" is an illusory one, since it has no firm foundations; it is temporary scaffolding that, without previous notice, will suddenly collapse, leaving him open to derision, humiliation, and mockery. This is a result of a tyrannical superego.

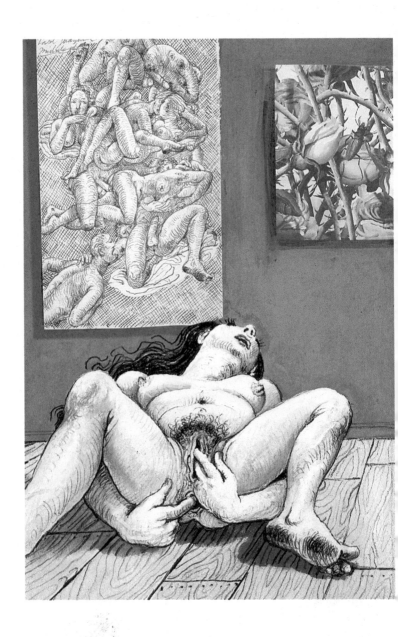

THREE

Punishable by external and/or internal law: public or intimate outcry

It may be more useful and effective to make a sort of classification of these sexual predicaments bearing in mind the question of whether or not they are punishable by law. This may provide us with clues about the internal processes that draw individuals who know of their vulnerabilities to seek power, control, and authority and, in so doing, risk being "publically uncovered", resulting in humiliation and "disgrace" that will have an impact both on them and on their extended family.

Obviously this is both relevant and linked to external power, since, as already stated in the section on encapsulation, it implies not only a split from the rest of the personality but also a private lie. What internal motivations lead a person to get a *public* position in which he could easily feel vulnerable and be subjected to threats of blackmail? It is possible that this sense of danger may actually increase the excitement that is being sought. At times it could easily trigger a life-or-death situation, as in the Houdini example. These individuals may be in positions of power and authority as a result of a very cruel and even sadistic superego, which has taken complete control.

Frequently we learn from the media, especially the tabloids, about such individuals being caught in public in the most humiliating situations, uncovering their deeply encapsulated "secrets".

In a way, the shocked response from society is a reaction to feeling tricked by someone who had appeared to be "so normal", as opposed to the expected monster. Nobody knew about it, not even those closest to him or who loved him.

Why is the shock so profound? The shock reflects the fact that these individuals have frequently been widely known for their very conservative and moralistic views. These views are for the most part most prejudicial and damaging to others – usually to those from minority groups and most vulnerable to abuse. The views emanate from what they really fear is inside themselves, and their mechanisms of projective identification are now flagrantly open to all.

What they were so vocally able to attack outside themselves was actually a part of themselves that was utterly loathed. As such it had to be vomited, expelled on to others. Their barely contained sense of self-disgust was a cover – like a hypocritical overcoat. From accusing others and being in a position of almost feudal power, they are now in the lowest echelons of society and are made objects of punishment and derision. They will either fall into deep depression or try without success to conceal the facts and, feeling trapped, will deny the facts even further.

Adopting a different perspective, we can see that the experience of "near death" actually works as a reassurance of being alive. (It is worth remembering the Houdini example.) Individuals in positions of public office feel trapped from the inside and the outside. There is a sense of double moral standards, of duplicity, which may precipitate further excitement at the service of the superego. The fear of being caught, along with the fantasised humiliation that would ensue, gets them into an unparalleled and overlapping position of simultaneous risk-taking and excitement. This adds to the erotisation of death as the last sentence.

As a matter of fact, when caught, despite enormous losses of all sorts, these individuals experience a great sense of relief at not being able "to get away with it" any longer. The true nature of whatever brings them much agony, pain, and suffering is now in the open, and they have a chance of being "judged" as they really are.

DECEPTION AND PORNOGRAPHY ACTING TOGETHER

I remember a patient who was referred to the Clinic because of his habit of using pornography as his only way of obtaining sexual gratification. He would pretend to be a fashion photographer and approached women in the commercial heart of London, telling them how beautiful they were and that he was prepared to offer them jobs posing as models in advertisements for expensive ornaments. After this grooming, he invited them to a conference room at a nearby hotel, where he asked them to uncover their breasts, which, he explained, was essential for the selection process. Most women acceded to his suggestions, even when it involved fondling their breasts and kissing their nipples. Afterwards, he would apologise and invite them to have a cup of tea before they left. He said that no one had ever complained. However, instead of being grateful for their tacit forgiveness, he was rather demeaning of them. According to him neither his mother nor his sister would have humoured such requests, and his "victims" deserved his dishonest behaviour. In our work together, we later revealed that this was a demonstration of his contempt towards women as a consequence of feeling ostracised by his absent father and of his mother and sister's intense relationship and denigration of him.

Some of the essential characteristics of pornography have to do with a complete absence of empathy towards the other person, so much so that the other person is non-existent, becomes "it", just a fetish. There is a strong dehumanisation in that the other person is seen only as a part-object there to fulfil sexual desires.

This could be accompanied by concealed hostility, as the following example clearly shows.

MURDER CRAVINGS COVERED UP AS SELF-HARM

This example shows that even when a woman speaks of being dangerous to others and openly boasts of this, there is a deep accompanying undercurrent of self-contempt and hatred towards her own body.

A twenty-six-year-old patient told me how she fantasised about butchering the bodies of unknown men. In these fantasies, she would "draw" them to her under false pretences to obtain their cooperation in fabricated activities, while all the time harbouring murderous designs. She boasted of being "extremely dangerous" and even claimed to have killed a few people, but it was impossible to know whether these claims were real or mere fantasy.

What was her real problem? She ate to the point of extreme obesity. She cut and burned her own body, and most of these wounds were inflicted on her erogenous zones. This pain caused her great sexual relief. Other wounds were inflicted on exposed areas of her body, visible to all. To begin with, she tried to rationalise her behaviour, claiming that it was a way of protecting others from her murderous desires. However, when I started to explore her claims at a deeper level, she reluctantly admitted that the obvious disturbance and discomfort that she elicited in others through her exposed (sometimes open and raw) wounds gave her a great sense of gratification and pleasure. She said she was trying to punish everyone by harming her own body. But, of course, in her statement she overlooked the damage she inflicted on herself. Such sadistic and masochistic actions are a typical trait of female mental disorders, although at times these are present in adolescent boys who experience much vulnerability and a sense of isolation. The pain experienced is an evidence of being still alive.

On one particular occasion, a motorcyclist reacted furiously to the reckless way she was driving. Suddenly, and with difficulty, she managed to get out of her small car. The man stopped, looked amazed, and said with utter contempt: "Your body is an ugly sight – obscene – especially considering that in the third world people are starving. It's pornography." Suddenly her turbulent anger was replaced by bitter tears. She was furious but felt trapped because she realised at that moment how the way in which she treated her body was patently seen not only as an angry act against herself, but also against everyone else. In the "homicidal spirit" that led her to this confrontation, it was easy for her to see that she could not persist with her old litany: "If someone tells me it's wrong to burn and cut myself, I say that I see nothing wrong with doing it. My body belongs to me and is exclusively under my control."

Through this example we can see how women can actively participate consciously or unconsciously in hating themselves for being women. This motorcyclist, totally alien to her, had interpreted her unconscious motivations correctly! Furthermore, and less clearly, he may have been reacting in an unconscious way against her strong desires to murder all men.

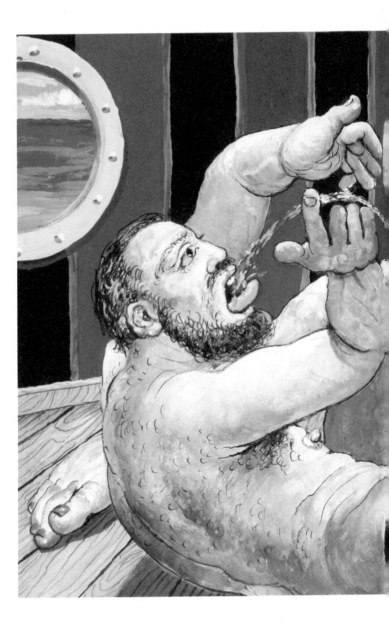

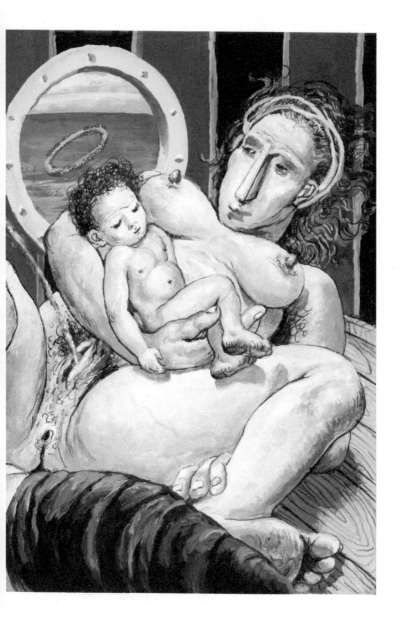

FOUR

Rape and sexual abuse
in childhood

"I AM DETERMINED TO BE A GOOD-ENOUGH
MOTHER – EVEN IF IT KILLS THEM"

This is an unimaginable scenario about the condition of a woman who was born as the outcome of a most violent rape.

"Doris" has attempted to kill her own four children and herself on at least three occasions. She is convinced that they have been harmed from birth because she had passed on to them the genes from their grandfather – the rapist – and that they are also psychologically damaged as a result of her being a bad mother when she felt depressed and unable to care for them. She does not experience regret about these attempted killings: on the contrary, she feels a great deal of shame at not having succeeded. She is adamant in saying that she would prefer them dead rather than endure the suffering she has gone through. She has never envisaged including her husband in these killings.

She had previously been an inpatient at a medium secure unit for around ten years, where she was treated with medication and a long series of electroshock therapy.

Brief background

Doris is the product of a violent rape in a country engaged in a civil war, occupied by the political opposition. Her father is unknown; he was first thought to be of a different nationality, but it later transpired he was an informer citizen from the same country.

> In her own words: "My birth was my family's shame. . . . When born, I should have been thrown out of the window into the river at the back of our house. Sadly, no one bothered."

> She was brought up in her grandmother's home, an all-female household, and was constantly subjected to humiliation and denigration by her mother and aunts.

> When Doris was eight, her grandmother, who had been her "one and only good-enough relationship", died. Shortly after this her mother got married, and almost immediately her new husband began physically and sexually abusing Doris. He also got his male friends to join in her sexual abuse. She got locked out of the house at night and was left to wander the streets.

> At age fourteen, she became pregnant, though not being completely aware of this, but she remembers vividly that she was in the bathroom when the baby came out. Her stepfather, who was presumably the baby's father, was with her, preventing anyone from coming near there. When he saw the baby, a boy, he took him away from her. A horrific scene

then developed, which he forced Doris to watch: he wrapped the baby boy up in newspaper, poured on petrol, and then set fire to it.

Soon after this, she left home and started working in a special school helping children. She then decided to train as a nurse. (It is not unusual to find that a traumatic background leads to a "vocation" to work with a difficult population.)

Later on she met and married an Englishman. They moved to England and had four children.

To start with, she managed the household and the care of her children in an adequate manner. However, unresolved grief eventually caught up with her, and a few years later, following her mother's death, she attempted for the first time to kill her children and herself.

This attempt could be interpreted as being "forced" to give up her mother as the "bad object" from infancy and to take it onto herself to become the "bad mother".

A second attempt took place ten years later, following her hysterectomy. She began to be chronically depressed, being treated with antidepressants. She refused to talk and did not get out of bed for almost four years. She was treated with a series of electroshock.

The third attempt took place following some gynaeco-logical repairs, after which she became uncommunicative, refusing to eat or drink. This time she tried to poison her children by offering them tea laced with her husband's pre-scribed tablets (the children were by then twenty-seven, twenty-four, twenty-two, and seventeen), and then she took an overdose.

It was after this that she was detained under Section 3 of the Mental Health Act, 1983 and was transferred to the Regional Secure Unit for observation and treatment. She again had electroshock treatment, and somehow her depression seemed to lift. She often became violent, breaking windows and objects in the ward and throwing things at members of the staff. On one occasion, she destroyed all her previous medical reports. She also remained intermittently suicidal.

As after her first attempt to kill her children, memories and flashbacks began to assault and torture her mercilessly. The killing when she was only fourteen of her first-born baby boy, whom she secretly called Richard, still remains consciously the main focus of all her concerns and preoccupations. This trauma is responsible for her survivor's guilt.

She feels she is not allowed to survive him, and her four live children are to face the same fate. After all, in her mental representations, they are not only born of her body but are parts, extensions, of her own body and mind. As she gets better, this nightmarish imagery revisits her more ferociously than ever, with increasing suicidal ideation and homicidal feelings being left behind.

All her attempts to kill her children were executed in the same way: as a mother in her feeding role, she did it through poisoned food.

Referral

Initially Doris was diagnosed as having a severe personality disorder, later on as severely chronically depressed, and eventually as suffering from severe post-traumatic stress disorder. As such, psychotherapy was considered a possibility and she was referred from a medium-secure unit to an

46

outpatient psychotherapy unit for assessment of suitability for analytic psychotherapy. In the referral letter, there was a request for an assessment regarding the following very relevant points:

» as to whether this patient could be helped by having psychotherapy and, if so, what type of therapy;
» as to whether there was an increased risk of her killing herself; and
» the level of risk of any further attempts on her children's lives.

I decided to offer the patient a series of diagnostic consultations in order to provide us with a sense of the pace needed to explore the development in the relationship created from our different meetings.

She started weekly psychotherapy with me for five years, already aware of my impending retirement from the NHS. The following is a brief summary of her five-year period of psychotherapy:

> For the first three years, as she was a patient at the medium-secure unit, which was two hours away by road from our Clinic, she would be brought to the sessions in an ambulance, escorted by two nurses.

> As positive changes were achieved, she was given permission to have weekends at home with her family, and over time these visits increased in length and frequency.

> Three years after the start of psychotherapy, she was released from the medium-secure unit and began to live at home with her husband. From then on, she began to come to her

sessions on her own and of her own volition, using public transport.

During her period of therapy she brought much written material, including her own poems and dreams. In all these she shows that, despite being psychologically damaged, she is sensitive and creative.

At this time, Doris became a grandmother, when her daughter had a baby girl. Throughout she kept in consistent contact with her children, and she sees her granddaughter regularly and has a close relationship with her.

A plethora of insights are gained and much is to be learnt from somebody who has experienced so much violence, deeply enmeshed in sexuality and procreation, from the moment of conception onwards.

I believe that violence and the prediction of future violence are different for the two genders. Body, sexuality, and violence are inevitably intertwined, and physical, biological, and anatomical attributes are primary factors in the making of violent acts with a plethora of symbolisms and affects that are at times shared by men and women but are at other times clearly distinct. It is those distinctive characteristics that I would like to address, referring to women as a whole but specifically to Doris.

Our own female attributes in relation to fecundity, our capacity to get pregnant and become mothers, is pivotal to the comprehension of violence in general. After all, we are the ones who carry the babies in our own bodies and attend to the ministration of their bodies. We have invested so much in our mothering enterprises that we want to get the best results. Yet, at times, we feel suddenly assaulted from within by the realisation that we may not be able or feel equipped to deal with all mothering requirements. Our own emotional legacy, despite our best intentions, can easily interfere in our carrying out this in a consistent caring way, and it is then that we are not able to stop violence taking place.

What is the meaning of being the product of a brutal rape, especially where the ensuing baby is a girl? What inner objects populate her internal world? What are her mental representations? In her mind, does she experience that being a woman she is like her mother, the object of a rape and, as such, a weak, dominated, savaged, inert female body left behind from an orgy of a man's violent and sexual gratification? What, indeed, is the idea of a father in her internal world, who in a brutal fashion mindlessly leaves his seed behind?

Although there are, numerically speaking, far fewer women involved in crimes of violence, it is important to remember that there is much more violence at home than in the streets. And it is not only women who are the victims of domestic violence; at times, they themselves may become the abusers of their husbands or partners. But let us not forget that it is children who are the most vulnerable members of the family, and they are the recipients of much violence from both their mothers and their fathers and are also witnesses of parental discord acted out in violent fighting.

At times, women get involved in acts of violence that are very different from those committed by men. For example, the violence is often hidden away, taking place in the domestic sphere, and is born out of women's frustration. It is then aimed at those who are the dearest and closest and the most vulnerable – the children.

I have on several occasions observed young women who have suffered severe sexual abuse who experience a need to produce a baby, sometimes in a repetitive, compulsive fashion. Behind such pregnancies there are many conscious and unconscious motivations linked to finding evidence that their insides have not been utterly destroyed by the abuse. Each baby becomes the evidence of the young women's inner goodness. However, the validity of this "evidence" is short-lived since it is "external", and the horror of their inner world has not changed, so the process starts again.

It is essential to understand these violent processes as part of a multi-generational cycle of violence and abuse created at least two generations ago. This understanding would pre-empt facile moral judgements, and effective plans to break the cycle could be implemented.

Some thoughts on a psychodynamic understanding of Doris

Doris's suicidal and murderous actions are consistently related to issues to do with maternity and associated losses.

The death of her grandmother – the one stable figure in her life – may have left her not only totally desolated but also unable to experience any grief, especially since she had been constantly humiliated by her mother and aunts. The appalling succession of sexual abuse incidents inflicted subsequently on her by her stepfather and his friends may have led to a manic defence, a way of distancing herself from what was happening, replacing the "forbidden" grief. She may have experienced becoming the sexual object for all these men as identification with her mother at the time of her mother's rape.

Doris's sexual abuse culminated in her giving birth at the age of fourteen to a baby boy who was then murdered by her stepfather, his father. In her mind she becomes the re-enactment of her own birth when she sees herself as the hated baby, an object of savagery and barbaric behaviour. Unlike her the baby dies, whereas she continues to live.

This woman's predicament shows that through her homicidal attempts, she may be trying to protect her own children. She may have felt so overwhelmed by the shame of her own birth that she could only preserve her self (as a psychological entity) by sacrificing her own body and those of others created within her body.

Are these attempts motivated by survivor's guilt, or are they altruistic in nature? After all, what she had in mind was to save her children from the life she herself had. She wanted her children to die, just as she wished she'd been killed when she was born. She resents and repudiates her mother for not having done this, since she experiences herself to be a bad object, the outcome of a brutal rape by the most despised political public enemy.

There are, paradoxically, other challenges to the understanding of this patient: for example, how has this woman been able to mother four children in their early infancy without any gross misbehaviour? One could speculate that her "one good relationship" to her grandmother until the age of eight facilitated some healthy identification with her during that period that was responsible for her mothering her babies without any serious complications.

This "good-enough experience" may be responsible for her accepting the offered therapy, experiencing me as the enactment of her grandmother that she effectively used later on in becoming a grandmother of a little girl.

The psychotherapy went through different phases, during which I could see her emotional growth and physical bodily changes.

First phase: Fear of being suddenly dropped or rejected and the needs to be reassured.   At first Doris was bewildered at having been accepted for therapy, and I was constantly challenged since she assumed that very soon I would get fed up and give up on her.

> In the session just before the first Christmas holiday, Doris repeatedly demanded reassurance that she would not be rejected and that I would return.
>
> At the end of sessions, she used to refuse to leave.
>
> She used to get very angry at my silences: "Why are you not prepared to answer my questions?? I answer your questions. I don't know how to deal with your persistent, perturbing silence. Punishment?? There can't be any communication if there's no foundation to establish mutual trust. Can we come to an understanding between us: Will you let me know when you are livid with me and why? Will you explain what to expect?"
>
> She would bring all sorts of drinks, especially those heavily sugared ones that would jeopardise the diabetes she had developed, so she could check on my being alert to this fact.

She was obviously feeling and representing her lack of trust about my capacity to "feed" her properly. It also represented her feeling uncontained and uncared for.

Second phase: Open transferential aggression against her fear of dependency.   Earlier on, in facing distress and frustration, Doris reacted either with excessive anger and impulsivity or by becoming depersonalised, "spaced out", numb, an obedient automaton.

52

A new phase began in which enormous anger directed at me in an active way took place, which, I believe, had to do with her having an incipient sense of trust in me. She used to get irritated and later on became quite explosive, throwing things, like pens and paper clips, at me. At times, her hostility was hidden under a veneer of concern: "I don't want to see you when you aren't well. It's no good for you or me. You were not well last week, and you looked at me eyes dull yet ablaze with irritation!"

After she learnt of her daughter's pregnancy, she became even more agitated. She told me that if she could openly talk about her own experiences and her "awful" feelings about her daughter's pregnancy, they would make me feel revolted and, ultimately, I'd have no option but to reject her. As my interpretations and understanding of the negative transference became clearer, she began to think, as she very acutely observed, that the "therapist is the rapist". I was experienced as being too penetrating for her own good. Intense hatred and envious feelings were explored in the sessions. She could hardly tolerate my interpretations, and she often attempted to leave the sessions feeling furious with me. This was immediately superseded by guilt of a very invasive quality in which she made a "maternal" offer of taking care of me.

Third phase: Pains of growing up. Doris began to look forward to her grandchild's birth, and this was marked by a period of contentment. Her physical appearance had changed a great deal since she first came. She had been overweight, almost obese, and walked very slowly and in a rather robot-like manner. She had now not only lost weight but also her whole appearance had dramatically improved, her gait had become lighter, and she appeared much better groomed, looking younger. I saw myself, in general, behaving as a mother of a rebellious adolescent girl, observing the metamorphosis with pleasure.

After her granddaughter's birth, she would bring me pictures of herself and her granddaughter together. She became more placid.

A process of double identification began to take place, with herself being granddaughter and grandmother in the past and in the here-and-now. She began to allow herself to some extent to enjoy and to develop a growing relationship with her granddaughter. There was a genuine quality of taking care of the little girl and tremendously appreciating their bonding.

Doris began to talk with a sense of reality regarding her granddaughter's physical and emotional growth, in that she was already aware that "very soon the baby will walk away from her in search of other, more attractive things in life".

In listening to her, it seemed to me to be an appropriate time to make an interpretation that she had already been conscious of: the fact that a similar time is coming for us. Actually she *is* the baby who will walk away from me because of my impending retirement. This is in striking contrast with her previous "belief" that I would be a lifeline for her, to be there with her until she dies. Previously, on getting to know of the inevitability of the ending of therapy with me, she became listless, agitated, and angry. She told me that she dreaded her future life and that in a concrete way my retirement might mean her own retirement from life. She wanted to know if I am going "to put her right" before I go, or otherwise what or whom I was going to offer to her.

On my return from the summer holidays, I found out that she was now living permanently at home with her husband. In her first session she was rather confused and told me how, on her way here, she had got lost in the station where she had to change trains.

I noticed that she looked much more contained, and I remarked on the fact that she was not so agitated and was much more relaxed, which she was able to accept. She was ready to depart promptly at the end of the session. She also said that this time it had all been all right, that she could see that I was not angry with her, and then she left.

Fourth phase: Making contact with reality. Doris began to experience a constant preoccupation about her marriage and her awareness of her husband's complete detachment from her and everybody else, although he had always been seen as the "good man" in the family. He very much resented her improvement because one of its important outcomes was that she began to assert herself, to own not only her own voice, but also her feelings and ideas. This was the first time that conditions had been created for her to use and develop her own mind, or for her even to have a mind at all.

In a way, it also became a sign of mental sanity in her being able to be in touch with the mental torture and not to regress to the "automaton" state that she went through after the second homicide/suicide attempt, when she remained in hospital completely uncommunicative and isolated, a condition for which electroshock was required.

Even her homicidal and suicidal attempts had gone almost unnoticed. Her husband was the martyr, the one who "stands" for her and always takes care. This becomes so unbearable that there is always a possibility for her to go back to a state of profound depression and uncommunicativeness, turning her back into the "automaton".

The process of identification with the aggressor that dominates the lives of people who have been abused becomes rather entangled here. The two men who appear more ostensibly and significantly in her early life are extremely violent and sadistic, and both have been sexually attached to her own mother. Her biological father is responsible for her generally hated and repudiated birth. Her stepfather is responsible for her further denigration, her sexual abuse, and, later, the murderer of her first child. Are both amalgamated into one? Violence, sexuality, and sadism are all the ingredients mixed up in her psychological makeup. Her choice of partner, which appears superficially to be an unusual one, in that he can offer stability and support but simultaneously can't stand her being able to communicate her own feelings, becomes a sadistic one. It is interesting to note that she had never been charged and that her husband had elected to remain an apparently supportive and loyal family man but who had consistently refused to take anything seriously.

* * *

Not all traumatic events can be integrated into experience: there is a limit to how much these very traumatised patients can take in. Some experiences will remain untransformed in their minds.

This has also made me think and discuss with colleagues about modifications in psychotherapeutic techniques when working with patients who have suffered severe or very early traumas in which symbolic thought is often absent. How much and for how long can we venture with these patients to make interpretations that, although accurate, may lose all therapeutic value because patients may experience them as penetrating and violating and, as such, render the patients' unable to take them in and digest and process them? Indeed, how much is one cajoled or forced during the therapeutic process to become some sort of perpetrator? I believe that one should not hide away from interpreting the negative transference, especially in the initial phase, when patients badly need the recognition and acknowledgement of their negative experiences. On the other hand, the therapist should be on the alert as to how much patients could take in order to remain the therapist and not become The-Rapist.

A VIGNETTE FROM ACTING AS AN EXPERT WITNESS IN FAMILY COURTS

Despite my long experience of more than thirty years of working with severe psychopathology at the Portman Clinic and earlier on at the Henderson Hospital, I had managed to keep myself away from court proceedings for various and complicated reasons, not least a great fear of being grilled, persecuted, and humiliated by different QCs. This came to a halt when I was approached in a rather confrontational way by a *guardian ad litem*, who, having read my book *Mother, Madonna, Whore*, told me it was a disgrace that I had so far refused to give evidence in court. I decided at that point to accept my responsibilities and agreed to appear as an expert assessor of parenting abilities in family cases. This was a long and arduous journey that taught me a great deal about very disturbing and disturbed relationships in couples. The following is one such case.

"COUPLE FOUND GUILTY OF SEXUAL ASSAULT ON THEIR OWN CHILD"

I am sure that most, if not all, readers have seen headlines of this sort in the newspapers. Some may have reacted with incredulity, others with disbelief, but everybody with indignation and complete amazement. I think to myself: what a relief that Social Services are now much more aware that these awful situations of abuse *do* take place. This awareness makes them able to intervene when necessary, unlike earlier times when complete denial and disavowal interfered with any possibility of uncovering this kind of abuse.

I shall try, through the description of a woman, "Marie", whom I saw a while ago, to illuminate possible causes underlying such abuse, which I have called *malignant bonding*.

Marie sent to me for assessment of her maternal abilities

Some years ago, I saw Marie, at the request of a court report. I had to assess her due to her inability to take proper care of her child, a girl aged eight years, "Annie", who had already been placed with foster parents.

Marie presented herself as a prim and rather prudish young woman who looked younger than her chronological age of thirty-four. She had pleaded guilty, together with her husband, to two offences of indecent assault against their own daughter.

Initially I agreed to see her for a five-session assessment at the Clinic and for her husband to be seen by a colleague. The latter was impossible to accomplish since by then she had decided, after much hesitation and difficulties, to separate from her husband. She had become aware, and was able to acknowledge, that she had unwittingly married a paedophile. In exploring her early history, her unconscious propensity to be an ideal candidate for grooming strategies used by a paedophile becomes understandable.

She is the youngest child in a family of fourteen children and described her birth as a "happy accident" since she was the only girl and her next sibling was ten years older than herself. She always felt like a little princess, but as the diagnostic sessions unfolded she began to have flashbacks of being the victim of sexual abuse by all of her brothers. This abuse had been totally unnoticed by her parents, who were either too neglectful or too old to take care of her.

She told me that her problems had started when she met what she carefully described as her ex-husband. At the time of their meeting she had been involved with somebody else her own age, but as soon as she met this man she was immediately attracted by his manliness, charm, and easy-going, confident nature. He was eighteen years her senior, and she liked the idea of him taking care of her, such as going on outings in his car. All this was quite new to her since her previous boyfriend was unable to do any of this.

It seems to me that in her relationship with this older man a much earlier pattern in her own family life had been re-enacted, perpetuating the pattern of being the young, uninitiated woman considered much younger than her chronological age. It is possible that she behaved in a rather infantile, childlike manner, a pattern that originated from her unexpected birth, which may have been an important or crucial factor for this man, later on recognised as a paedophile, to be attracted to her.

A month after meeting him, she decided to move in with him, despite some objections from her parents. A month later, she got pregnant with Annie, and they decided to get married. In talking of her marriage, she gave the impression of not having a mind of her own, but, instead, was always attentive and acquiescent to her husband's wishes and wants. After a long period of incredulity at what transpired to be her husband's hidden motives in his courtship of her, she is now bitter, and believes him to be a chronic paedophile.

Marie breast-fed Annie until she was three-and-a-half years old; she knew that this was too long, but she got a lot of comfort and enjoyment from it.

It appears she found the mothering process very difficult, unable to help their daughter, who began to exhibit many behavioural problems that began to escalate, especially when she started school and was unable to concentrate. Annie had always been a very bad sleeper and had severe eating problems, and Marie had taken her to a number of different doctors. The school reports identified these issues, but the parents did not follow them up seriously.

Annie by then had discovered a strong liking for horses and used to go with her father to the stables to take care of them. Marie feels devastated at the later realisation of her daughter's early sexual abuse by her husband, which she believes had begun to take place at around the age of three or four during their time together at the stables. It was here that, years later, her husband was found guilty of sexually abusing other young girls. It is evident her early and constant use of denial applied not only to her own tacit participation in Annie's abuse but also to acknowledging to herself the severe nature of her husband's psychopathology. This becomes even more obvious when exploring his early detection and appearance in court. For example, when he was sent to prison, she could not stop her tears and sorrow at the thought of his not being able to see their daughter for a long time in light of his fondness and care for her.

She told me that she has been thinking a lot about Annie's abuse by her father and had become aware that there had been a couple of times when Annie had approached her about this. At the age of six, Annie had asked her in the kitchen whether it was possible to have a baby if her father's "willy" had gone into her tummy. On another occasion, at the age of five or six, her husband complained that Annie was telling a lot of lies to the other children about having sex with Daddy at the stables. Her own response to Annie was to say: "You mustn't say things like that".

Now she feels devastated about this, because Annie might never be able to confide in her following her early scepticism and disbelief. The disclosure came about because two other children who were at the stable complained about her husband's inappropriate sexual behaviour towards them. The police came the following day to take him from the family home and to interview her. This was the last time that she saw Annie for over a year, since she was immediately placed with foster parents.

Later on, Marie told me how her husband had got her to cooperate with the making of pornographic videos, including with their daughter. She was rather cautious in talking about this. Incidentally, it was only through her contact with her husband that she enjoyed sex for the first time: she had been unable to obtain any sexual satisfaction with her previous boyfriend. However, as soon as Annie was born, sex became absent from their relationship. After a while, her husband began to persuade her to do other things to improve the sexual side of their marriage. By then he was working as a part-time photographer, at times doing "page-three" type pictures of young girls.

In describing her involvement in pornographic videos with her husband, she told me that he cleverly engaged her interest in a very gradual and slow way. Had he told her from the beginning that he wanted to take pictures and videos of her wearing underwear, she might have been shocked and would have been able to say no. But the way he did it was seductive, slow, and escalating, in exactly the way a paedophile would groom a young, uninitiated girl, wooing her persuasively to gain her full consent. He began to tell her those other children, especially older girls, wanted to be part of those videos. She was captured by the thought of being on the stage and eventually posed in suspenders, which led her to believe herself to be a model. She was given strict instructions by her husband where to get the appropriate lingerie for the occasion. He also seduced her into the idea of having a video of a scene of a happy family, with mother, father, and daughter together. Her husband then asked her to cooperate with him in making videos of mother and daughter in inappropriate sexual scenes, to which she acquiesced.

Some time after this, Marie's husband told her that she was too old to be in the videos, and that it would be the last time he would use her. This was the last straw for her, but soon after this the whole situation was uncovered and he was arrested. Even then she was very sad about him and felt "responsible" for his imprisonment.

A long and extremely difficult period of psychotherapy took place when she was able eventually to acquire some insight about her own "contribution" due to her vulnerability and the previously denied episodes of being sexually abused by her older brothers.

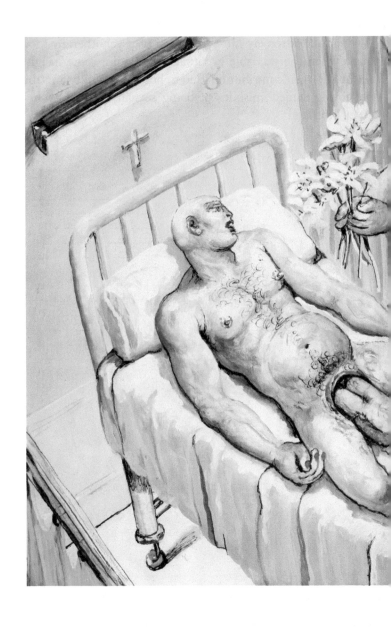

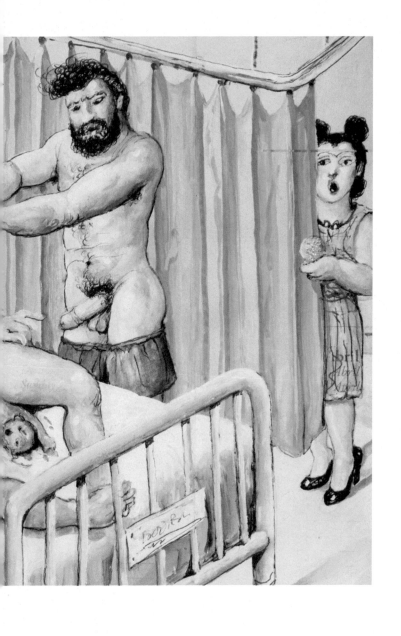

FIVE

What women have that men do not

It is truly amazing that women have for so long and so effectively been considered inferior to men.

Many feminists would consider Freud's penis-envy theory of 1908 to be responsible for this, but he was just following a long-standing tradition going back to ancient times. Although women were clearly central to the reproductive role, it was not invested with a superior status. Women were merely the soil, and men provided the seeds.

We can move from there to Freud's theory of the Oedipus complex, the desire in both boys and girls to have sexual relations with the parent of the opposite sex. This was easily resolved for a boy, who would desire the mother, but what about the girl? How could she get her own "independence" from her mother and become her own being? For Freud, the Oedipus complex was resolved in little girls when they fantasised having Daddy's babies inside themselves. As such, the "solution" was provided by the "procreation factor".

The penis symbolically gives males a sense of power and superiority that women could easily envy. But penis envy has been overrated: it represents not so much the physical organ as the male position of dominance in the world. We are often committed to using mythical or prejudicial views where we see men always in charge of erect penises and always able to impregnate any woman of their choice. We tend to forget that some men are subjected to penises with a life of their own, that do not respond to conscious desires, and we also tend to ignore that some men are sterile. They live a miserable double life, experiencing a tremendous pressure to perform with "cockiness" and arrogance to constantly demonstrate their sense of "superior" masculinity.

What has been overlooked is that women who feel in an inferior position try in a vicarious but vigorous way to achieve their own fantasies of power through their own reproductive organs and, furthermore, to act them out. Young women feel awkward and insecure in dealing with their powerful feelings about the tremendous physical and mental changes taking place, and sometimes they lack support from their mothers about their sense of femininity. After all, while some mothers of adolescent boys show off with them and obtain narcissistic gratification when mistakes are made about their relation-ship, the same mothers, with attractive adolescent daughters, feel put down by men's complimentary remarks about their daughters. The fresh beauty of young girls' bodies leads to a tremendous sense of competition as mothers age, especially as menopause approaches. Again, we are not talking about just one organ, as is the case with boys, who, when comparing themselves with their fathers, may feel inadequate and small, thereby accepting that father is in control. Fathers are rarely in such open competition with their sons.

The adolescent boy has an easier transfer of attachment from mother to another woman than does the adolescent girl, since the boy does not need to change his first love-object. The girl, instead, has to make the switch from attachment to mother to attachment to father. If she is then rejected by father, she may look for revenge in dreams of pregnancy.

The essential point lies in women's capacity for procreation, the expression of which is fundamentally different from anything men experience. This capacity drastically affects not only women's emotional lives, but also the mental representations of their bodies and, concretely, their physical bodies, albeit for a fixed period of time.

The second phenomenon, related to rhythmicity and biology, is "the biological clock". It is especially important in adult decisions about motherhood, particularly when "time is running out".

The inner space and the biological clock are different phenomena, but their effects intertwine. In women's lives, sometimes one is more important, sometimes the other. In adolescence, the "inner space" tends to be the more important of the two in relation to fantasies about pregnancy, while later the "biological clock" can be more dominant. At menopause, the two come together.

It is strange that so much writing and theorising has been devoted to penis envy, to the point that female bodies have been forgotten in this regard. This is the *real* equivalent to male castration since its aim is to destroy what is most envied – the capacity for procreation, to create a new being.

We must learn from envy and what it involves regarding the other sex and the other gender. Envy of the penis and envy of the breast and the womb are to be integrated together, and this union is responsible for much destructive envy when it is carried to the ultimate consummation. Both kinds of envy are the triggering effects of what is to come eventually with its further awareness. It is the explosive realisation that both female and male organs are together in the act of consummation and entering a new cycle of emotional and physical maturity in the realisation of becoming parents.

This combination of different organs acting together in producing feelings of plenitude is in open evidence; it is painful to watch and can easily provoke extreme and disturbing responses in the onlookers. For example, although it is known that pregnancy can trigger off violence and that pregnant women are prone to physical abuse by their partners and also by strangers, it is not often thought that a pregnant body could constitute a source of humiliation in that men feel infinitely inferior and excluded even if they were responsible for the pregnancy.

This is the primal scene *par excellence* and leaves the panorama open to vulnerable, immature individuals in a most curious predicament: even those men responsible for the pregnancy may be subjected to powerful and opposing emotions. Consciously they are proud and excited at their own potency at having impregnated their partner. But, as usual, things are not that simple: some men return to the position of being the humiliated and excluded child. Violence in pregnancy is traditionally seen as a male response to feeling shut out of the woman's body and intimacy, as the woman's insides are now otherwise occupied and he is made to feel redundant.

There are also vulnerable women who feel undeserving of becoming pregnant or who have enormous fears of producing unhealthy babies because of their own inner fantasies of not being whole or "complete".

I have become increasingly aware of all the complexities

attached to the female body, its unique attributes, and the psycho-emotional political elements surrounding women's existence, the patriarchal law and women's experience of lack of power in a man's world, and her unique access to domestic power with its potential for abuse: the fact that the baby's emotional and biological progress depends on its mother's ability to care for it.

We are familiar with the notion that the breast is usually associated with desire, envy, and the tremendous rage of jealousy, especially in connection with breastfeeding. This is yet another scenario for the primary scene in that a third person is witness to a most beautiful and unique bonding. As already mentioned, the mother–baby unit is at a biological–psychological peak when the mother is ready with her breasts filled with milk just as her baby is being awakened by hunger. Both parties get together, and a world of bliss is open to them.

It is no wonder that this experience is strongly felt by most men. The most insightful ones are able to openly talk about the confused experience they go through while witnessing such an intimate scene which is a miracle of nature – an unequalled symbolic and concrete linking of desire, nurturing, an achieved sense of fulfilment, and a great contentment shared by mother and baby.

He and his partner had previously been participants in the sensuous and sexual feelings derived from touching, kissing, and caressing the breast. Now, he is left as a witness to the union between the two people closest to him, his partner and his own baby. But this time she is no longer his partner but is solely functioning as a mother. The previous sexual breast has now become a feeding, life-sustaining one.

Freud described women's sexuality as a "dark continent", but in pregnancy darkness is no longer there: it is pretty luminous, and flagrantly undisguised, that for that woman to be impregnated is the consequence of her having had sex. Here we encounter another problem, which is the tacit association of sexuality with maternity.

Now it is this unique combination of the power of the sexual union, with its vitality and vibrancy, that is the subject of so much envy, leaving in the shade the traditional penis envy or its counterpart – the forgotten or not easily acknowledged envy of the womb.

SYMBOLIC ATTACKS AGAINST MOTHER'S BODY

Over the years I have heard patients talking about the severe traumas and emotional deprivation experienced during their early years and the ill treatment inflicted by their carers – usually their mothers. It became apparent that their acting-out behaviour could be easily associated to those early traumas, with an enormous, intense, and unconscious urge for revenge against their mothers. These patients had been subjected, often from birth, to their carers' unpredictable and bizarre behaviour, which included all sorts of abuse, sometimes sexual, leaving them defenceless and powerless.

As grown-ups or adults, these individuals may appear to the outside world to be completely normal, but a hidden component of their personality remains quite defective.

I believe this to be related to the faulty sexuality component in their personalities creating an enormous fear and even terror of becoming dependent on or being on intimate terms with anybody else, because their unconscious hatred towards the early carer deeply interferes with their capacity to love.

These individuals are not able to choose love objects but are compulsively subjected to part-object relationships where nobody is seen or experienced as a whole, or seen as a different being. "Making love" is replaced by "making hate", since the intimacy usually found in so-called normal adult couples is absent; instead, there is only momentary relief from sexual anxiety.

There is an unconscious need to take control and get revenge against authority and its agents. These agents or people in authority are the mental representations of those who in these individuals' childhood were in charge and responsible for welfare – in other words, their parents and, more specifically, their own mothers. Now as adults, they do not experience freedom in their object relationship – on the contrary, they respond in compulsive ways to fixed scenarios and, despite themselves, succumb to bizarre sexual behaviour, since it is the only way to obtain some relief and a reassurance of being alive.

This acting out is enacted in concrete ways, but at other times all sorts of symbolic equations are being used. For example, the following clinical vignette demonstrates the complexities attached to being a victim of maternal incest in that the patient has a feeling of entitlement to act out provocative, offending sexual behaviour with persons in authority, representing her abuser mother.

A COMPULSIVE NEED TO SYMBOLICALLY ATTACK THE MOTHER'S BODY

In the seventies, a patient of twenty-eight was referred to me by his employers, a City bank. (It was a revelation in itself that a City bank then could be so perceptive of the possibility of unconscious motivations.) He was the bank's "bike" man, responsible for carrying money to and from different places, and had been detected stealing spanners from boxes of other bikes. Police found he had stolen thousands of spanners.

In the interview with me, he tried to make sense of his unlawful actions by explaining that he was a handyman and that the price of tools was subject to inflation, a clumsy and inadequate explanation that pointed to other motivations. In describing his actions, he talked with a great deal of embarrassment mixed with excitement. "When I see another bike being parked, I feel overcome by an extreme curiosity to look inside its box. I can't help myself. I start sweating, my heart pumping, and I just have to take the tools. Then I feel at peace, a great sense of relief. I feel great. Later I start feeling confused, ashamed, and guilty."

His statement is similar to that of a person suffering from high sexual anxiety, showing a quality of urgency, a cycle that involves increasing anxiety, fighting against it, eventually giving in and gaining sexual relief, followed by a sense of shame and guilt.

This was a young, well-groomed man still living with his mother, a domineering narcissistic woman who had never allowed him to lead his own life. When the police came to get him, her first reaction was: "What shall I do if you take him away. I can't be on my own." He had never had any relationship of any sort other than with his mother, and he lived in complete isolation.

This man's criminal offences were the expression of his tremendous sense of social and sexual inadequacy, which, in turn, was the product of a deprived and depraved early childhood. His father had been absent in the war, and his mother had a severe narcissistic borderline personality, using the patient as a fetish for her intense emotional neediness and making him behave as her confidante.

Our psychodynamic view was that the patient was drawn to the motorbike because it represented the mother's womb, and the spanner the father's penis, which he felt the imperious need to take away. As such, he felt he was attacking his mother's body from the fantasised union with father's penis, through which he found sexual relief and even a sense of solace when empowered by grabbing the symbol of his father's penis and dislocating mother and father from that union.

This particular symbolism is also present in incidents where breaking and entering into houses takes place. Those responsible are usually youngsters who, once inside, indulge in all sorts of revolting behaviour, including urinating and defecating on things, leaving the house in a complete mess, but stealing nothing. This leaves the house owners feeling humiliated, violated, and angry and the police completely disconcerted and puzzled. These are sadistic actions against mothers' bodies symbolically represented by the house they have broken into. It is perhaps not at all odd that these particular antisocial actions are much more often perpetrated by men rather than by women.

Some violent actions, including homicide, may have roots in early experiences of humiliation and shame. It is crucial to make the important connection that all acts of violence are preceded by inner experiences of humiliation.

INCEST AS AN OUTCOME
OF THE FAMILY DYNAMICS

In the following case of paternal incest, the roots of which became clear only after years of therapy, we realised that this was the outcome of extremely complicated family dynamics.

When they married, my patient's wife already had a girl from a previous partner. Following the cot death of the child, a boy, the wife had with my patient, she became psychotically depressed. Grief and bereavement were not allowed to be experienced. She was emotionally and psychically unavailable to my patient. The incest subsequently committed by my patient started as unconscious revenge against his wife, which was represented in his sexual abuse towards her daughter from a previous union. As such, it also encompassed his enormous rage and envy towards her fecundity of which he received no benefit as a father.

According to Kleinian theories, during the schizoid position the baby experiences an enormous split in relation to its mother and is only able to experience her as a good or a bad breast over which the baby has no control. It is constantly attacked from within with a most persecutory imagery. But as this is projected outside onto her, the baby inhabits a persecutory universe, becomes paranoid, and may wish to retaliate with violence, akin to how a violent partner behaves towards his pregnant/preoccupied/abandoning wife. This is superseded by the depressive position, when the baby can integrate both positive and negative aspects of the breast within itself. The baby is then also able to differentiate between itself and its mother as a different being.

I believe that people afflicted by bizarre and extreme urges have been unable to reach the depressive position; instead, they remain in the paranoid-schizoid stage, and the splitting goes on and on (encapsulation again). They see the m-Other as the attacking object, using projective identification, and as such they are constantly attacking mother's body in symbolic ways. This becomes a mini-kit of psychic survival.

My suggestion is that such people – whether male or

female – are still in the stage of intense hatred towards the mother's body and her mostly unavailable feeding breast. This produces an eternal sense of insatiability, frustration, and anger, which creates a sense of entitlement to nurse a grievance with the concomitant need for revenge. My contention is that this revenge is not just directed against the unavailable breast, which is outside their control. The vengeful, sadistic attack is actually against the pregnant body that encompasses the successful union between the two partners and whose final product, as opposed to expectations of being loved, cherished, and treasured, is easily discarded as a cumbersome, demanding, and unwelcome new baby. This new baby is the future seriously disturbed individual – no wonder, considering the amount of revenge and sadism experienced, which is then acted out later as adults.

We are able to observe these attacks during analytic treatment when we, as therapists, experience a tremendous sense of uselessness and powerlessness.

With women, the problem is that they cannot distinguish their own bodies from those of their mothers and so attack themselves or their babies in a repetitive chain of events that persists over at least three generations.

For men, the female body, but especially the pregnant body, is a reminder of the capacity of the woman to change from being a sexual partner to being a mother, and as such she becomes, in his mind, unavailable for his own emotional, physical, and sexual demands or requirements.

Both men and women are unable to control such envious feelings, and the outcome is the experience of impending annihilation; it is then that they fall into bizarre acting out, which keeps them alive. This acting out is experienced in a compelling way, and, as such, repetition is always required, because the intention, which is symbolically to kill the mother, is rarely, if ever, achieved, given the tremendous fears associated with killing the one who gives birth. But this is coupled with intense envy as this idealisation of the womb meets the denigration. The object, so much idealised, is intensely hated and is subjected to constant sadistic attack.

Obviously there are always exceptions, and these can reach gigantic and drastic proportions, as happens with serial killers, who may have been victims of maternal incest. They usually keep a very low profile, never creating problems in school as children, and suddenly and completely unexpectedly react in most violent ways.

FEARS OF HOMOSEXUALITY AS A DEFENCE AGAINST MATRICIDE

Sometimes sexual predicaments and hidden violence overlap, as in the following brief case history.

> A young man of twenty-three first came to treatment because of fears of being homosexual. After a year of individual psychotherapy, he left treatment having overcome his fears.
>
> A few years later he was back because he had suddenly and unexpectedly experienced violent fantasies against all women, but particularly his mother and, later, his girlfriend. When alone with his mother, he was constantly assaulted from within with the desire to kill her with a kitchen knife, and he found it extremely difficult to curb this strong impulse.
>
> He had achieved an intimate situation with his girlfriend but now felt the urge to hurt her. In an obvious attempt to do so, he had had a one-night stand with another girl.

He described a recent dream, in which he had his fist inside a woman's vagina and was punching vigorously. When he started to enjoy this process he became aware that he was disintegrating – first the hand began to dissolve, and later the whole body was annihilated.

This dream represented his fears of being destroyed by a woman if he becomes close to her. His fear of homosexuality had been a protection – replaced later by a deeper fear, expressed through violent fantasies – against women, who he felt had previously damaged him, indeed almost emasculated him. It would not be a surprise to learn that his mother had subjected him to a series of repeated physical humiliations with extreme intrusiveness and immediate rejection, which had left him in a complete state of confusion and persecution.

ENVY TOWARDS ONESELF AND OUTRAGE AGAINST MOTHER WHO GAVE BIRTH

I discussed earlier the case of Doris, who made several attempts to kill herself and her four children. She was aware of her intense hatred towards her mother, and she was also trying to kill all that she experienced as goodness inside herself because she was envious of her own capacity to produce healthy babies. In more severe cases, mothers suffering from a psychotic episode may be successful in committing homicide.

In pregnancy, the woman is able to turn her hatred of her mother, as symbolised in her own procreative body, towards herself and her own unborn baby. This is exactly what all these sexual manifestations have at their core: the attack from both females and males against the female body or its creations – the babies.

The so-called perversions are a survival "mini-kit" fending off the death instinct, and they are the outcome of the envy and rage engendered by the awareness that the sexual union that brought them into the world ceased to do any emotional nurturing after the conception of this new being.

There seems to be an obstinate tendency to see women as the weak sex, always the victims and never the perpetrators of sexual assault. Women have always been held to be incapable of effecting their own perverse sexual designs, and young boys were reckoned to be the only ones to enact sexual fantasies. I believe that many theories of female sexual development are ill-founded, partly through their being based on a need for an ever-present "earth-mother", a woman who has been so idealised, or perhaps even idolised, that her faults are overlooked. She is portrayed as powerless in the penis-envy dilemma or, according to the new feminists, the victim of social attitudes, even perhaps contemptible because she seems of less importance than the male. It looks as though we have all become silent conspirators in a system in which, from whatever angle we look at it, women are either dispossessed of all power or made the sexual objects and victims of their male counterparts. We do not accord them any sense of responsibility for their own unique functions, deeply related to fecundity and motherhood, and liable at times to manifest themselves perversely.

Despite advances in feminism, the "law of the father" remains the dominant model of Western psychological and cultural analysis, and the law of the mother continues to exist as an underdeveloped and marginal concept.

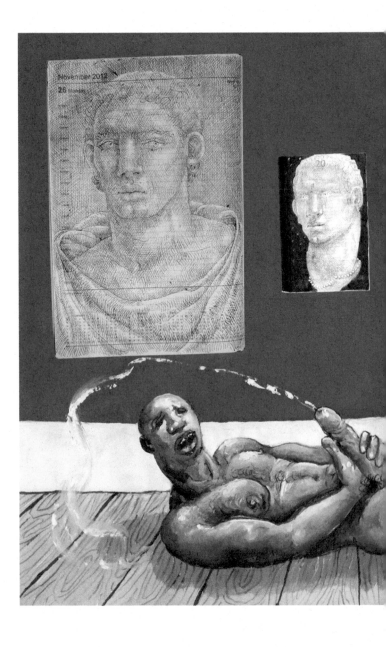

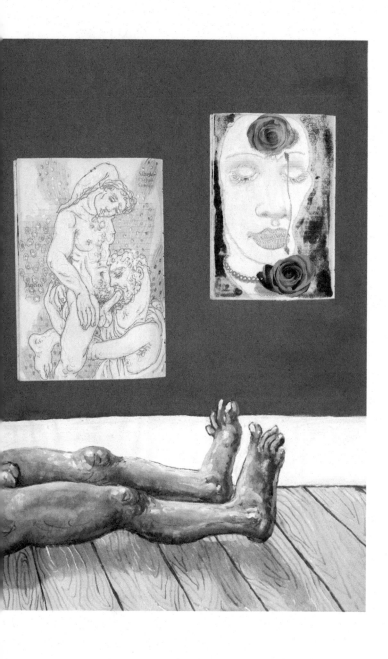

SIX

A question of pornography?

Pornography is a very difficult concept to explore, possibly because many subjective and objective factors are at play concurrently, within a very broad range of different types of pornography. This complexity has increased considerably with the advent of the Internet.

The difficulty is also due to the ambiguousness of the concept. For example, if we look for "pornography" in the dictionary, we see that the key concept is "obscenity". If we look for "obscene" we find the notion of "lewd". Hence, little additional understanding can be expected from any dictionary, especially if we consider the temporality of the term. What was considered "pornographic" in the cinema fifty years ago is now more or less just a "daring scene", which qualifies as suitable for children under fourteen. The Marquis de Sade's *The 120 Days of Sodom*, banned in Britain in the sixties, has recently been published as one of the Penguin Classics.

Like all of the sexual themes explored so far, pornography too easily evades the awful complexities of relationships.

I remember some decades ago, when I was still (although not consciously so) quite naïve and without much clinical experience, attending an international conference in Wiesbaden, Germany, entitled "What Is Psychotherapy". Simultaneously in London, a famous court case for obscenity was taking place, linked to the principles of censorship, which then was quite severe in England. The case related to a book widely read by then, *Last Exit to Brooklyn*, a novel with a language raw and direct on hot topics and taboos of the time: drugs, crime, rape, homosexuality, and violence not only in the streets but also in domestic settings.

This book was described as "a journey to the end of the American Night" and "a portrait of a society without love". It had already been banned in Italy. In Britain, the jury had to decide whether the book constituted pornography; if considered as such, the publishers would be deemed guilty.

During the conference we had dinner on a boat sailing on the Rhine where I was fortunate to sit at a table with three major international psychiatric authorities, all liberal and full of understanding for all antisocial problems.

At the table were Professor Morris Carstairs from the University of Edinburgh, Dr Maxwell Jones, creator and director of the therapeutic community at the Henderson Hospital in Sutton, and Professor Jurgen Ruesch, a famous Californian psychiatrist who was an authority on communication. He was one of the originators of the concept of the "double bind", meaning a situation in which a person is confronted with two irreconcilable demands or a choice between two undesirable courses of action.

The three of them kept up a very entertaining and I

would say even passionate conversation about the concept of pornography and how this could be applied to *Last Exit*.

I was a keen, silent witness to a rich discussion in which all versions of, and theories about, pornography were put forth without ever reaching any understanding suitable to the novel. At one point the conversation became banal and childish, when Jurgen suggested that the decisive factor in the book's judgement could be the number of offensive words that appeared in it – just as if everything could be decided by a mathematical concept and percentages. We parted feeling, I think, quite frustrated.

Back in my apartment in London, I was chatting with the contractor who was repainting our building, and at one point he asked about my conference. I took the opportunity to ask a very direct question: "For you, what is a pornographic book?" Without a moment's hesitation, he replied: "Ah, that is unmistakable: a pornographic book is one I can read with just one hand."

And, of course, his answer, despite or perhaps because of his lack of academic distinctions, was insightful and clear beyond any doubt. Because it is the interaction between imagery and bodily reaction that makes pornography. Pornographers, to be successful in their aims, must know and correctly guess the images and language – or whatever is being used – that will stimulate and provoke an irrepressible sexual arousal.

PORNOGRAPHY AND ART

In 2013 the British Museum had an extraordinary exhibition on Pompeii and Herculaneum, with sex as a specific topic, making explicit that the phallus was one of the objects most represented in the daily life of the ancient Romans. Since it was assumed in those days that phalluses were the "messengers" of good luck, houses contained cooking utensils and ornaments shaped as phalluses. The streets of Pompeii were adorned with stone phalluses for people to touch and, consequently, bring them good luck.

However, despite the explicitness of the exhibition, the effect was not one of sexual excitement, possibly because of the quality and beauty of all the objects. These are erotic figures linked to art and, as such, are unable to cause sexual arousal.

The relationship between art and pornography was clearly enunciated a few years ago at a professional discussion on pornography at the Tavistock Centre for Couple and Marital Relationships when Howard Jacobson, a renowned English novelist, asserted: "No man masturbates watching the Sistine Chapel!"

This could alert us to another facet of the crucial difference in the elicited opposite response to a beautiful artistic creation where explicit sexual scenes are in view. These produce in the viewers an inner admiration and recognition that leads to "enlightenment" on the spiritual plane. This is not really pornography: it could be called eroticism, which is the exaltation of physical love in art, but it is not pornography.

The pornographic is ugly, coarse, obscene, something that works simultaneously as an assault and a sexual stimulant for those who are mentally vulnerable, wrapped in a severe depression of which they are totally unaware. In a way, the viewer recognises and identifies with the sadistic nature of the creator of the pornographic image, a sadism usually aimed at a woman.

In Roman times there were no inhibitions about art

with sexual scenes, nor any kind of censure or repression. The contrast between the lack of inhibitions of that period and the Christian society of the eighteenth century became apparent when excavations uncovered the erotic art of Pompeii; the strong repressive pressure of what was understood as public morality led to these discoveries being locked away in the Archaeological Museum of Naples, in a separate part of the museum called the Secret Cabinet. It was not until 2000 that these historical and artistic wonders were fully presented to the public.

It is relevant to remember here two of Freud's books, *The Future of an Illusion* and *Civilization and Its Discontents*, in that both focused on the influence of Judaeo-Christian religion in the origins of sexuality.

Whereas the phallus or penis is usually openly on display when pornography is the theme, the fact is that most pornography originates from the female body. Interestingly, the body used is generally beautiful and young: it is a body for which there is no old age, nor even the merest hint of the process of aging. It is always not only an attractive body but one capable of reproduction.

THE SEXUAL ACT

In Ricardo Cinalli's drawings throughout this book, the voyeur becomes the central character, and we see him or her incorporated in the intimacy of the sexual act and, at times, even included in it and an active participant. This is what we call "the primal scene".

It is relevant here that while Cinalli was producing these drawings, he was undergoing a course of chemotherapy: it was a period during which he was fighting for his life.

"My drawings replace desire, and in this way I can say that desire moved from the body to my art; in the process of drawing you forget your body! They are personal and intimate; reflections of my Eros and Thanatos."

His drawings emphasise that the sexual act is to do not only with pleasure, but also with pain and, ultimately, death.

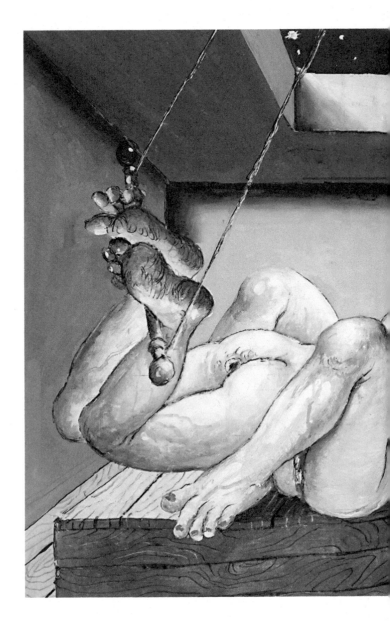

SEVEN

Insights gained about female prostitution from Hollywood films

I would like to focus on some of my own observations on Hollywood motion pictures depicting both public and private scenes of female prostitution.

For a long time my interest in films depicting some of the sexual predicaments seen in the consulting room has been focused on one of the most important features of female sexuality – that is, the madonna–mother–whore split and its relevance to Hollywood, especially in relation to sex, morality, and the role of women in films. This inevitably led me on to a concomitant of the madonna–whore syndrome – namely, the private–public dilemma that is characteristic of both prostitution and films. In the first case, a situation can arise in court in which a woman who works as a prostitute is confronted with the law and charged with procuring. Compare this with the second case in which a film star is adored by an admiring audience in a cinema. Both scenarios involve the "taking up of a role". The "as-if" personality so usually found in adolescence is present in both prostitute and film star, but whereas the former suffers ostracism and opprobrium if her trade becomes publicly known, the latter benefits from her enterprise and gets public recognition and appreciation. It is in the nature of prostitution that whatever is considered to be private in the production of intimacy becomes profitable and public. This particular trait is also in the nature of the cinema in which the audience at times finds itself a voyeur or "peeping tom", watching highly intimate situations in the public arena of the movie house.

The stereotypes of Eve and woman in her various roles as virgin, mother, or whore have had immense influence on the everyday lives of almost everyone in the societies exposed to them. Hollywood representations of art and myth reflect the attitudes of society with all its prejudices and stereotypes. Hollywood has also helped to create them.

Film script writers, as talented people with a keen eye for human behaviour, have observed the manifestations of all sorts of sexuality and have wanted to include them as true to life, but this insight has been in tension with society's (and often their own) splitting of the images of female sexuality.

In the twenties and thirties, Hollywood tried to deal with sex in two parallel ways: first, through a code suppressing sexuality; second, by titillating the audience with sexual fantasies of a pornographic type. Woman was seen more and more as a commodity to be sold for the purposes of lust, eroticism, and pornography. This was the "public–private" view. On the other hand, in the "private–public" view, the woman was the star never to be seen pregnant or having children. It was as if fecundity and nurturing, though incontrovertible proofs of consummated sexuality, could paradoxically enough inhibit the sexual fantasies of prospective viewers. Sex was rarely connected with pregnancy and children. Female stars in their daily lives were not allowed to have children, and sometimes not husbands.

Hollywood reinforced the connection between money, intellect, and sex. In general, money and intellect are supposed to belong to the male and sex to the female, and each deserves and usually gets the other.

The Hays Code (or Production Code) – which censored films through a series of guidelines to which producers needed to adhere – was written in 1930, after many attempts by the Motion Picture Producers and Distributors Association to develop a self-censorship system. The 1934 decision came about for many reasons: the Catholic Legion of Decency organised interfaith opposition to Hollywood; early thirties gangster films such as *The Public Enemy* were criticised for making gangsters sympathetic characters and for suggesting that illegal activities could result in economic welfare; the early thirties' "kept-woman" film cycle raised concerns about women living comfortable lives by exchanging sexual favours for economic security.

The Production Code was not without its contradictions. Interpretation of films included attention to "proper compensating moral values". Good (moral) characters would be rewarded with happiness (true love, success), while bad (immoral) characters would be punished (death, dishonour, unhappiness). Thus, the ending of a film was privileged: films could represent immoral or illegal activities to a limited extent, provided that the narrative was so designed that the ending would properly "compensate" the characters in terms of the Code's moral values. The Hollywood "happy ending" is inextricably tied to "appropriate" moral and social values.

Sex was connected with tits, not brains. Sex was then associated with immoral, sordid issues, and it was only acceptable if indivisibly associated with marriage. Women left the bedroom and went to work in offices, and for those who behaved "properly" happy endings were obligatory. That is, the girls who knew how to restrain themselves from any sexual, "impure" desire were rewarded with a happy marriage. Those who dared to contravene that "law", and indulged in pre- or extramarital sexual affairs, had to face severe punishments such as dramatic, sad endings involving serious accidents. Still, the fact that women were provided with capacities outside the bedroom was a desirable side-effect of the Hays Code.

The Hays Code had the effect of making "proper" women out of "loose" ones, and in so doing it also affected women's sense of humour, since it denied the possibility that women as well as men could enjoy a sexy joke. Humour became the monopoly of the male gender, although the sexy joke was successfully used by witty women such as Mae West. Her famous remark: "Are you carrying a gun or are you just pleased to see me" was soon banned, since it denoted not the socially "acceptable" women's "penis envy" but, rather, Mae West's own acute insight that the distinction between the sexes should be regarded in a complementary way.

In the fifties, the professional virgin emerges, being the embodiment of all the mistrust and hypocrisy legislated into the Production Code and frozen into a smile, the tease whose every romantic ploy is directed towards marriage and security. Apart from the sexual repression of the fifties, another phenomenon was present but hidden away, and it appertains to male homosexuality, which was not only not allowed but harshly punished. This produced other side-effects in films of this period. The actress became, then, for certain directors, like John Mankiewicz and Billy Wilder, not just the symbol of woman but the repository of certain distasteful qualities that certain homosexuals writers, like Tennessee Williams and Edward Albee, would like to disavow. There is a massive projection onto the female protagonists of narcissism, vanity, and fear of growing old which they are horrified to find in themselves.

In the sixties and seventies, women's sexual liberation and the acknowledgement of female sexuality paid an excessive price. Women were back to "sexy" roles but without the stardom. They were cast in undermined and debased roles in which they did not have any qualities but those attached to sexuality. If women are so aware of their sexuality and can dare to express openly what they want, "let's give it to them or even better let's force it into them" seems to have been the "sentence" meted out by male "judges". As a consequence, rape and sexual violence became the rule.

It is against this background that I would like to contrast and to use as clinical vignettes two films. The first, *Camille*, was made in 1936 by a "woman's director", George Cukor, with two of the most famous stars of the time, Greta Garbo and Robert Taylor. The film, based on Alexandre Dumas's *The Lady of the Camellias*, has all the dramatic overtones of romantic love, but it adds an unexpected twist that makes possible the change from a vulgar happy ending to a beautifully dignified one. The unsurprising price paid is the heroine's death in her deeply repenting lover's arms. So much for man's capacity to get "instant" insight about true love only when confronted with his lover's death. This is also accompanied by a sudden switch from a debased and denigrated vision of his dying lover into one of idealisation and forgiveness in view of her inevitable death.

The second film, *Klute*, was made in 1971 by a most intelligent and sensitive director, Alan Pakula, with two box-office stars: Jane Fonda, as "Bree", and Donald Sutherland, as "Klute". The film demonstrates not only some of the stereotyped attitudes that society has of prostitutes, but also some of the characteristics of the men who pursue them. In tune with the "revolutionary", "subversive" times, the establishment wealthy businessman is the unexpected sadistic rapist and killer. However, despite the differences between the cultural and social mores of the two decades, the relationship between the main protagonists in the two films is very much the same: a loving, unique one, which is discovered or revealed to both female characters, Camille and Bree, for the first time. So much for the romanticism attached to the Hollywood touch, in which it is only when women are at their most vulnerable or sick that they are able to bring out the best in men. Incidentally, money in exchange for sex is absent from both relationships.

In both films, the directors show understanding and cunning. Both Marguerite and Bree go through serious ill-health crises in which their lovers, Duval and Klute, take care of them. It is particularly poignant that those scenes are full of recently discovered tenderness and new love, evocative in their use of gaze and touch, of the first love between mother and baby. In other words, there is a pre-Oedipus complex situation at work, which requires the active presence of the Father, the Law, since it is violating the "natural" relationship between man and woman with the implied threat to the paternal union. I shall come back later to this point.

In *Camille*, Armand's (Marguerite's lover's) sister provides both the excuse for the father's intervention and the image of the virgin in opposition to the whore, represented by Marguerite. This contrast is even more clearly drawn elsewhere: Marguerite's protector, the Duke, with whom she has a "platonic" relationship, sees in her the living image of his dead, virginal daughter. When Armand's father forces Marguerite to give up his son to avoid imperilling his daughter's "proper" marriage, he says of the latter: "She is young, beautiful and pure as an angel. She is in love, and she too has made love the dream of her life." So, obviously, she is the one who deserves to be loved. Marguerite then begs him: "Kiss me as you would kiss your daughter." This scene shows Marguerite's internalisation of patriarchal norms, despite her marginal position. This is a key point since it will lead us to the world defined by the Father, the Law, the patriarchal law, which is considered to be higher than any association with the Mother, woman.

Marguerite and Armand's relationship is not an exchange between prostitute and client, it is a true romance. He falls in love with her after learning that she is very ill. Actually, this fact makes the love story possible, since it will provide the perfect ending. Marguerite defies most conventions attached to prostitution, but the price she pays for this romantic defiance is to fall ill of consumption and die young. Armand is full of devotion and jealousy and is possessive of her. He does not pay for "her favours"; on the contrary, he "unknowingly" benefits from her trade. She loves him and shares all her anxieties with him, including those of her profession, such as not being allowed to show her feelings and being "just a thing" to her clients. She tells him: "You were the only person with whom I'd sensed from the first I could think and speak freely. Naturally, we [courtesans] have no friends. We have egotistical lovers who spend their fortunes not on us, as they claim, but on their vanity. . . . For men like these, we have to be cheerful when they are happy, hale and hearty when they decide they want supper, and as cynical as they are. We are not allowed to have feelings, for fear of being jeered at and losing our credibility. Our lives are no longer our own. We are not human beings, but things." Dumas's statement grasps beautifully and accurately the prostitute's predicament.

(Incidentally, he has also unwittingly provided us with the meaning of the Kleinian term part-object, in a painless way.) The same feeling is conveyed in *Klute* when the heroine in a session with her therapist says: "I would like to be faceless and bodiless and to be left alone."

There are two central issues in *Klute* which give away that Bree and Klute's relationship will not follow the typical prostitute–client pattern. First, Klute appears to be a "straight" guy, who can resist her attempts to seduce him and give him a "freebie". However, the real give-away is when she starts talking of herself as a "neurotic", suffering from nerves, phobias, and being scared of the dark, hence disclosing her areas of vulnerability to Klute.

Female prostitution involves both sexes, and the men as well as the women have problems that are not always obvious. In more ways than one, double standards are at work. This is not surprising, since a contract based on money is entered into, and the two parties are in some ways accomplices but in other ways opponents.

In *Camille*, Prudence (a close and older friend of Marguerite) offers Armand words of wisdom, when she says: "Kept women always expect that there'll be men around who'll love them, but they never imagine that they themselves will fall in love. Otherwise, they'd put a bit to one side and, by the time they're thirty, they'd be able to afford the luxury of taking a lover who pays nothing." She offers an interpretation of the dynamic which implies that the woman is so strongly convinced that she will always control the situation that she can imagine no change in it.

Klute from the very beginning, even before the credits start, shows the dichotomy between the good woman–wife, who knows nothing about possible bizarre or "kinky" sexual activities in her husband and the existence of the prostitute

(Bree) who has been the receiver of obscene letters from this "respectable" man. The film at times of suspense plays a recording of the prostitute's voice enticing her male clients with a single sentence which is heard over and over again: "There is nothing wrong – do it all – the only responsibility you have to me is to enjoy yourself."

This is quite a different voice from that of the superego, which can become tyrannical, inconsistent, and sadistic. What a sense of relief it is, even if for a short time, for the client to listen to this "commandment" over and over again, which grants him permission for whatever "kinky" bizarre activity he has in mind to afford him sexual gratification. Added to this, he is told that his enjoyment is all that is required from this transaction.

A revealing insight appears in a session that Bree has with her therapist where she tries to describe her trade. She says about the punters: "They are usually nervous – that's fine because I'm not, and I know what I am doing." She adds what she experiences about herself and says: "You don't have to feel anything, you don't have to care, you don't have to like anybody." "You just lead them by a ring in their nose in the direction they think they want to go." "You control it." "You call the shots." "I feel great afterwards." At this point the therapist asks: "Do you enjoy it?" "No, but this has nothing to do with morality, but I came to enjoy it when I learnt that it makes me feel good, because I feel I have some control over my life." So, as we can clearly see, the woman in the course of her work as a prostitute gets rid of her own fears of losing control and her own anxieties by observing them in her client.

However, the most revealing situation takes place in a third session with her therapist when Bree, in talking about her amazing discovery of sexual happiness, says candidly: "I just find it baffling, I enjoy making love to him. I feel like breaking it off. I keep hoping that it's going to end. At least I had control before. I'm not setting anything up, I just feel that the sensation is flowing from me naturally to somebody else without setting any traps." This makes it really clear that an object-relationship is replacing the part-object one previously described.

In talking of Klute and his care of her when she was over-dosed, Bree says: "He's seen me horrible, he's seen me mean, he's seen me ugly, he's seen me whory and it doesn't seem to matter and he seems to accept me. And having sex with all those feelings is new to me and I just wish I didn't keep wanting to destroy it." Again, here we can observe the deep split and ambivalence about this newly acquired sense of trust. It is so frightening to trust, because this actually means for those who feel so vulnerable and weak a renewed betrayal of the new relationship that will include humiliation, deception, and a total and utter rejection – all emotions they have lived with all their lives. We are able to observe a deep split between genital sexuality as a living – or, shall I say, loving – force and what appears to be sexual but actually corresponds to much more primitive stages of development, where pregenitality pervasively dominates the whole picture. Achievement of intimacy with another partner through sexual intercourse – the norm – is replaced here by a release from increasing sexual anxiety through a bizarre action or situation which is in itself inexplicable not only to others but also to the person himself.

In prostitution, there is a false understanding – that the encounter is only or primarily a sexual-genital one. Again, the dynamic of "sex now, talk later" is in action. Both parties are actually involved in a compromise whereby the sexual mother is taken over by the strict mother, provider of bodily ministrations. This is why so many client–prostitute contractual situations are completed without any physical interactions, let alone sexual ones of a genital kind.

A process of projective identification takes place within both parties' minds in an attempt to resolve this primitive splitting. The prostitute now becomes in fantasy a mother with a young child – her client – submissive under her control; simultaneously she is a whore who is supposed to provide that "youngster" with sexual gratification. This is made possible by a process of depersonalisation, by a mutual and reciprocal process of splitting and by the denial of emotions that occur as a result. In prostitution the client at times becomes the mother and the prostitute the child. At other times the client becomes "the dirty old man", with connotations of dirt associated with money or faeces corresponding to a pre-oedipal stage. At other times, he is the "sugar daddy", easily associated with orality, sugar, and milk; in other words, the client becomes, in symbolic terms, a mother who is able to feed the woman–baby–prostitute, to satisfy any whimsical needs she might have.

A process of triangulation is demanded, which is offered by a strict and punitive superego – the Law – a symbolic father who is called upon to perform his duties. He is expected to extricate both parties from an unhealthy association and to create some sense of order. That is the role that Armand's father plays; later the Duke, through his mourning, re-enacts it symbolically, casting Marguerite as his dead, virginal daughter.

Prostitute and client are re-enacting an "ideal", illusory, and collusive situation in which the symbolic mother–baby unit tries to get away from the husband-father, while they are both knowingly challenging the law–husband–father to prosecute. But the father colludes with his own gender in the application of the Law: the woman is charged, while the man and his emotional predicaments are dismissed.

The "strange man" who pays for the prostitute's favours is the deteriorated and idealised image of her father. The man in pursuing prostitutes is looking for a mother he desired as a forbidden sexual object; unable to obtain this sexual gratification, he has to content himself with a substitute maternal denigrated figure. She keeps alive the madonna–mother–whore split.

There are different kinds of female prostitution. I am here referring to women with a very low self-esteem. In order to get out of this "low", they start to solicit. When men appear and are ready to pay for their services, they feel enormously elated. Soliciting, then, is used as a "regulator" of their self-esteem.

There are some circumstances in which women apparently seeking money in a client–prostitute relationship are at a deeper level actually seeking punishment. That is the case with women who engage in prostitution with such recklessness that they are easily caught. When such women appear in court on charges of soliciting, they feel that the charge in itself will prejudice everyone against them and that nobody will bother to get to know about them, their upbringing, their emotional needs, and personal circumstances. Such is their despondency that, expecting no real understanding, they usually make the law enforcers collude with their inner persecutory needs, which leads to disproportionately heavy sentences. And, indeed, society feels so hostile, not only to prostitutes' actions but also to their inability to defend themselves, that it is unable to separate their actions from their personalities. Thus, sentencing sometimes carries with it an unconscious recognition of their actions and of their need for punishment.

This point is clearly demonstrated in *Klute* when Marguerite tells Armand of her meeting with his father in these words: "Your father believed implicitly in the conventional truths according to which every courtesan is a heartless, mindless creature, a kind of gold-grabbing machine always ready, like any other machine, to mangle the hand that feeds it and crush, pitilessly, blindly, the very person who gives it life and movement", and yet she has in fact accepted the demand of Armand's father and given up her lover.

Some women in prostitution experience a caricature of intimate relationships involving revenge. This revenge, which appears to be directed against socio-economic submission and a man's world, is actually against the mother. In these cases the prostitute's urge for revenge involves a desire to be in charge, and elation while with her client. This conscious control fulfils an unconscious denigration of herself and her gender, because she afterwards feels debased. In this state she is too depressed to harbour vengeful fantasies against men, as is usually stated. Actually, she identifies with her male client in his contempt for her and her own gender.

Most professions, regardless of how demanding they are of our time, emotional involvement, and physical strength, still leave us able to pursue separate public and private lives. In the intimacy of the latter, we replenish our mental and physical resources. This is not possible for women who practise prostitution; indeed, the opposite is the case. This aspect of their predicament becomes obvious when they appear in court, where their private lives are exposed to the public. Since their profession involves them offering and providing their clients with gratifications of a very intimate nature, their own private needs have to be ignored. Everything private becomes public, this being the nature of the conflict. Some women unconsciously hope that once their problems are acknowledged and in the open, help will become available to them. Unfortunately, help is only rarely the response.

In the late eighties and early nineties, stardom belonged to the glorified or sublimated version of male homosexuality in groups. Men were shown to communicate a whole gamut of feelings among themselves, to support one another without a tinge of rivalry, and to produce a wonderful climate of bonhomie. Men were portrayed as able to perform all tasks, whereas women, when allowed to appear, did so as nagging, frustrated, greedy creatures who could be seen as negligible and easily discarded. Films such as *Bringing Up Baby* were followed more boldly by *City Slickers* and *The Fisher King* in which the men supported and helped one another in painful processes associated with separation, loss, and bereavement, whereas the women were token representations of female inadequacy endowed with extreme clumsiness or with "sexual" overtones.

As we can see, it is rather difficult to provide a happy Hollywood ending for this particular subject, since a happy ending would be in itself a contradiction of the situation. But in films, financial not psychological profits are at stake. Interestingly enough, in 1990 we saw the box-office success of *Pretty Woman*, in which a golden-hearted prostitute meets her match in a highly successful businessman. He is isolated and emotionally empty, and the two of them enter into a process of mutual nurturing. The "happy ending" is provided by their marriage. It must be said that this is not a probable outcome to the situation – but perhaps, after all, marriage is no longer seen as a happy ending.

In the mid-nineties a more realistic, and tragic, ending takes place in a similar partnership in *Leaving Las Vegas*. This is no longer *Pretty Woman*, in which the punter is a successful, wealthy young man who can indulge in any fantasy except for the achievement of a real relationship. Here we encounter both characters desperately determined and intent on their own self-destructive quests, Ben having decided to kill himself by drinking and Sera by being exposed to daily brutalisation at the hands of her pimp. They are able to rely on one another in their resolution to kill themselves, with a tremendous sense of consistency. Both make reciprocal promises: Sera will never ask Ben to give up alcohol, and Ben will never ask Sera to abandon prostitution. Moreover, she offers herself as container for his addiction. When she is able to give up her pimp, who had abused her in all sorts of different and cruel ways, she is mugged and brutally raped by a gang of youngsters, representing her internal need for consistent humiliation and sadistic treatment.

The film brings alive an accurate picture of the miserable internal worlds that both characters are suffering. Degradation and denigrated parts of themselves play a crucial role. There is a compelling symmetry in both characters in which the victimisation of woman is no longer a prerequisite. Both characters offer a degree of equality in their miseries and vilification.

In the late nineties there is yet another change in which some effort is made by Hollywood to understand the complexities attached to human sexual behaviours.

Seeing *Happiness* has made me rethink, and I am changing completely my perception of the way in which sexual misbehaviours are or can be portrayed in Hollywood films. This 1998 film is a real breakthrough in the understanding of a sexual perversion in a most humane and compassionate way. The film is populated by characters who, under a veneer of normality and functioning as family members, are disclosed to have a black internal world with much loneliness and cruelty. Other aspects of their lives suddenly shock the audience, who feel assaulted with new insights, such as the solitary wanker who has to make pornographic phone calls to achieve any degree of sexual relief. Even paedophilia, of all imaginable perversions, is accessible to the point of being understandable. After all, most of us feel attracted to children, but our attraction is limited to their candidness and vulnerability, at times covered up by a façade of cheekiness. This is very different from paedophilia, where the degree of exploitation and sexual abuse is covered up as "grooming" of the children involved by the grown-ups. This movie has really made it. The main protagonist, who is a psychiatrist, is played in a most sympathetic manner, never sentimental, but crystal clear about the admission of both his inability to fight against the strong desire and the enormous pleasure he attains from abusing – not only that, but also his clear admission that he would do it again and again if he only had the chance. There is neither remorse nor guilt, only a cool and realistic acceptance of all these factors operating in his mind – even more so as the children involved, when asked, seem not to regard this as something that really hurt them. They are unable to recognise the spirit or the nature of the question.

When addressed as if somebody has *hurt* him, "No" is his answer. There is no glorification of the industry of abuse, just a clear and blatant statement of what it is like to be a paedophile. An ordinary man. If you want to call a shrink an ordinary man surrounded by a "warm and supportive family", of course all this is full of deceit, which again is beautifully performed in the film.

Hollywood has surprised me with this authentic, highly educational display of one of the most despised sexual problems ever.

EIGHT

Understanding versus judging murder by going to the opera

It is not by chance that professionals involved in forensic psychotherapy are fond of, or even at times addicted to, opera.

Operas portray life in passionate terms, with vivid, vibrant characters whose lives are lived to the extreme, to the extent of committing acts of violence as deep expressions of love, humiliation, shame, and hatred.

You may say that the characters are exaggerated or even caricatured versions of "real" people, but this helps us to understand deep passions – for example, when love is suddenly turned into hatred and violently enacted. It is in these scenes that the most brutal and violent sadistic behaviours are portrayed.

In this way, we (the operagoers) become silent witnesses to all sorts of extreme behaviour. In a way, you can say that operas are the sophisticated and artistic version of the tabloid crime stories that so fascinate people!

But – in contrast to those tabloid tales that elicit the dissociation of the reader from the perpetrator of those "horrid crimes" and, in so doing, give rise to an experience by proxy of virtue or goodness – operas inspire a search for understanding the motivations underlying such "savage" behaviour.

Opera, because of its art, wonderful music, and great productions, helps us in a unique way to understand what at times are too often called "irrational" crimes. The manner in which emotions are raised by opera helps us restrain ourselves from any prejudicial reading and, instead, encourages our understanding of and identification with the characters. This identification is catalysed through the creativity and artistry involved in their acting and singing, despite the discomfit this evokes. In this way, opera becomes an exercise in challenging our intellectual abilities and laziness and in gaining an insight into the most demanding predicaments that human beings encounter in their lives.

The following section intersperses case vignettes from my work with protagonists from the world of opera.

KILLING FROM A STRONG EXPERIENCE OF HUMILIATION

Billy Budd

Benjamin Britten's opera *Billy Budd* is able to offer us, beneath the superficial and easily attributable gayness and levity, a great example of a violent act – murder – committed by an individual caught in a position of utter humiliation and abso-lute vulnerability. The opera takes place in a ship exclusively inhabited by men, and for this reason it is usually categorised as a "gay" opera.

Billy Budd is a beautiful, benign, peaceful, and exemplary young man who suffers from a severe speech impediment.

This impairment, almost imperceptible at times, becomes severe in intensely frustrating circumstances.

Billy was impressed into service; he is inexperienced and rather naive and as such becomes an easy target for bullying and eventually malice, envy, and denigration. When unexpectedly the captain summons him, he eagerly arrives overjoyed, since he has just carried out good work and is expecting to be offered a promotion, with good reason.

The opposite happens: the captain tells him that, without any doubt, he is responsible for a mutiny and accompanying transgressions. It transpires that these accusations have been fabricated by Claggart, the Master-at-Arms, who is extremely envious of Billy's natural charisma. The other sailors had joined in an escalation of their bullying and fun at his expense.

Billy Budd is completely taken by surprise, and in this state of shock he is unable to defend himself or explain that he has nothing to do with this alleged mutiny. He is unable to voice his rage and becomes increasingly confused and incapable of expressing his justifiable anger. In a knee-jerk reaction, he strikes Claggart on the head with a nearby hammer; to Billy's amazement, Claggart falls to the ground dead.

This a great example of an extreme reaction of the most violent type coming from a person who goes from feeling noble to being misinterpreted and confronted with mockery and derision.

Lady Macbeth of the Mtsensk District

A similar scenario takes place in one of Shostakovich's operas, but this time the antagonist is a woman, and the victim a man.

Katerina is a young, inexperienced girl, unhappily married to Zinovy, a provincial flour merchant. She is not only bored but also obviously sexually frustrated. When her husband is away on business, she falls for Sergei, a new worker in their business and a notable womaniser. They begin a love affair, which is immediately all-consuming. She feels so strongly about him that she is naively convinced she is the only woman in his life, when in reality she is only one of many.

To safeguard the continuation of her affair with Sergei, she kills her father-in-law and her husband, whose body she buries in his place of work. When the killings are discovered during her wedding to Sergei, both are imprisoned in Siberia. Katerina bribes a guard to allow her to meet Sergei, who blames her for everything and mocks her for being so stupidly naive. She shares the same cell with another woman convict, a young and beautiful girl, Sonya. In no time Sergei declares his passion for the young woman and proceeds to make love to her, witnessed by Katerina. Ultimately, as a result, Katerina kills him.

This killing is motivated firstly by an enormous sense of disbelief, followed by tremendous humiliation at being made the object of mockery. The pivotal episode preceding the killing is Katerina's gift to Sergei of her last pair of new stockings, on the understanding that they will ease his pain; these he quickly gives to Sonya for sexual favours. When Katerina sees Sonya wearing her own stockings, she is possessed by rage, spits in Sergei's eyes, and kills him.

In this instance the stockings trigger off the murder, just as earrings are the trigger effect in *Wozzeck*, by Alban Berg, another opera in which murder takes place. In *Wozzeck*, a man murders a woman as a "resolution for feelings of humiliation". In this opera, earrings given by a lover outside their marriage are evidence of unfaithfulness. This plot comes very close to the case of a patient of mine, whom I shall describe shortly.

Wozzeck is a sailor, of low standing, who is constantly the

object of humiliation and derision by many different people and in various settings. His partner, Marie, the mother of their small son, succumbs to a sexual encounter with a Drum Major who gives her, in exchange for her sexual favours, a pair of earrings she has been admiring.

When questioned by Wozzeck about them, Marie says she found them. He doesn't believe her, but lets the subject pass for a while, until he steels himself with a knife and kills her, witnessed by their son.

In both operas – *Lady Macbeth* and *Wozzeck* – the triggers for the violence and killing are the gifts of fetishised feminine objects: stockings and earrings.

I was impressed that in the final scene in a recent English National Opera production of *Wozzeck,* the son, about nine years of age, instead of playing with his hobby-horse as in the original version, menaces the audience with imitation weapons, fully continuing the violence of the previous generation.

In two further extremely powerful operas, which portray strong, beautiful, and intelligent women, their husbands – the fathers of their children – are now in a quest for much younger women, which provokes murderous feelings towards the unfaithful husbands.

The first is *Norma*, by Gaetano Donizetti. When Norma becomes aware that Pollione, her partner and father of their two children, is showing signs of a lack of interest, her attitude towards their children is totally changed: she exclaims in deep sorrow: "My children – at times I love them and also I loathe them. They give me so much pleasure and so much pain."

When aware that Pollione has fallen in love with a young novice priestess, Adalgisa, Norma's first reaction is to hurt him in a most drastic way – that is, by killing *his* children. At that moment, her rage is directed towards him as the father of their children.

The second instance is *Medea*, by Luigi Cherubini. Medea is highly intelligent, in power, loved and in love. When Jason decides to abandon her for a much younger and more powerful bride, she is abruptly and unexpectedly dispossessed of all that she had. It is then that she becomes aware of the only power left to her: her children, who become the target for her revenge against their father. Medea skilfully and subtly hatches a plan designed to give as much pain as possible to Jason through killing their children. She feels justified in her actions, such is her agony at her own predicament, and manages to complete the terrible deed within the space of twenty-four hours.

Men and women behave in contrasting ways when encountering intense humiliation, and once more we are able to see clearly distinctions in the way they react. Whereas in men revenge is directed towards their partners or what they experience as the new love-object the woman has found, in women it is directed against their own acts of creation: their babies.

HOMICIDE IN REAL LIFE AS THE OUTCOME OF HUMILIATION

Now let us go from opera to real life, and a case vignette that could easily have been used as the subject of an opera.

> I saw "Tom" while he was still serving a life sentence. Before the murder of his pregnant girlfriend, when he was only twenty-one, he had no forensic history. Indeed, he had an exceptional work record and had been a conscientious and responsible individual.

120

He was living in the north of England with his girlfriend, with whom he was very much in love. One day, on returning from work, his girlfriend, while preparing dinner in the kitchen, confronted him with the fact that she was pregnant. At first Tom was overcome with joy, but this was quickly superseded by utter humiliation and shame when she told him that he was not the father, and that she had been seeing another man. Tom saw red; he was beside himself and lost in extreme rage. The next thing he remembered was seeing his girlfriend dead on the floor, surrounded by blood. He ran through the streets in heavy rain for hours and eventually found himself at the police station, where he confessed his dreadful deed. He was amazed to learn that he had used a kitchen knife to stab her thirty-two times in the abdominal area; his attack was aimed directly at the fruit of her infidelity with another man.

I saw Tom again years later, when I had to assess his suitability for outpatient treatment on leaving prison. He told me his early history. He was the seventh in a family of thirteen, and there was a gap of seven years between him and his closest siblings, both before and after his birth. He had constantly witnessed his parents' bitter fights, from which he used to recoil in fear. He began to create fantasies in which he rescued his mother from this scenario, taking her to a place where he would provide her with peace and solace. These dreams continued until he was age seven, when unexpectedly his mother began a new cycle of pregnancies.

We can imagine his sense of humiliation and shame at his mother's pregnancy and his jealous rage at his younger siblings. Is it possible that his own sense of impotence as a child was reactivated by his girlfriend's confession of being pregnant by another man? Furthermore, could it be that he unconsciously made a link to his father (another man) who had not only penetrated but also impregnated his mother (girlfriend)? When I mentioned to Tom the possibility of group therapy, he was horrified. Of course, group therapy would be too much like "home", being surrounded by siblings, and he was unable to take this on. Instead, he came regularly to his individual sessions for years, and we were able to gain insights into these links with his unconscious fantasy life.

There is an echo in this of Leo Tolstoy's *The Kreutzer Sonata*, inspired by Beethoven's piece of the same name. The story is a monologue by the only character we meet, Pozdny-shev, as he sits in a railway carriage on his return from a prison sentence. Prior to this he had seen his wife playing the piano in his own home with a violinist friend and, without any further thought, believed that they were making more than music together. The envy and rage that this fantasy engenders propels him to kill both his wife and the violinist. Although he sits alone in the railway carriage, listening to the hypnotic rhythm of the wheels, we are shown glimpses of the wife and her violinist, and we listen to the beautiful music created by them – the music that is responsible for Pozdnyshev's delu-sion and his still active fantasies of violence triggered by his subjective sense of humiliation.

In 2015 I went to the Sam Wanamaker Theatre to see *Kreutzer vs Kreutzer* under the assumption it would be a new production of the same play. I was completely taken by surprise and thrilled to see a completely new play (again by a woman writer!) In this innovative and compelling piece from playwright Laura Wade, two strands are entwined: Beethov-en's *Kreutzer Sonata* and Janáček's string quartet of the same name with Tolstoy's novella, *The Kreutzer Sonata*.

In Tolstoy's story, as I began describing above, a man confesses to a stranger on a train that he has murdered his wife in a fit of jealousy, convinced that she has had an affair with a violinist and that they were stirred on by Beethoven's stormy sonata. In this production the author approaches the tale from the point of view of the wife and "lover" (neither of whom has a voice in the original). The first half of the evening traces developments through their conversations, punctuating the story with the three movements of Beethoven's sonata for violin and piano. In this version of events, they do have an affair. In the show's second half, the same story is repeated, only this time the variation is a minor key and they resist temptation. Their dialogue is broken up by Janáček's intense, tormented quartet (written in response to the novella and empathising with the woman).

It sounds complex, but in practice it is beautifully simple. Both actors touch as they speak in light, often droll dialogue. It is the music, played with searing passion and exquisite precision by members of the Aurora Orchestra, that expresses more overtly what is happening between them and how they feel. In the first half, the violinist and the pianist (man and woman) pass phrases back and forth, join, follow and complement one another, and you notice more than ever the necessary musical sympathy between players. In the second half, the tone between the two actors changes and is now subtly strained with longing and fear; the four quartet members bend and weave with the turbulence of Janáček's music. The struggles within the piece amidst poignant snatches of lyricism and frantic bouts of agitation seem to speak for the characters.

Music, which Tolstoy saw as dangerously hypnotic, is crucial to the action, since sex was no longer part of their marital life. Sex was only allowed for the purposes of reproduction, and since his wife had been ordered for her health's sake to stop having children, sex had stopped. She goes back to an old passion of hers, the piano, and at his insistence starts playing duets with an old school friend of his. This provokes a tremendous jealousy, which escalates as the playing becomes more and more harmonious. At one point he says: "Timing is everything in music. Well, timing is everything in life." Pozdnyshev is excited to the extreme, with an almost religious ecstasy, when the pair play Beethoven's *Kreutzer Sonata*.

Having seen three productions, I was enlightened recently when I saw this play at the Arcola Theatre, and it became clear that Pozdnyshev's strong sense of entitlement to the killing of his wife stemmed from his feeling that he had evidence of his wife's "infidelity" – the point at which the duet has reached perfection.

It constitutes the evidence of her infidelity, just as when my patient, Tom, learnt that his girlfriend had become pregnant by another man. Both had a temporary feeling of entitlement to kill their partners. In the play, the wife had always been faithful, but her fate is nonetheless to be the victim of her husband's jealousy, just as Desdemona is to Othello.

NINE

Conclusions

The sorts of problems discussed in this book might respond to different therapeutic approaches at different phases of the perpetrators' lives in which antisocial and even criminal behaviour may be representing different needs.

We need not only to modify terms in the understanding of this process, but also to revise our therapeutic approach.

These patients do not always respond to psychotherapy: as a matter of fact, only a few do, and they need to be adequately diagnosed. Their treatment in all settings needs to be carried out only by experienced, well-trained psychotherapists for whom supervision is essential in order to function effectively. I am referring here to a therapeutic approach that involves proper management, accurate diagnosis, and being part of a working multidisciplinary team in which the cooperation of all involved is essential.

The basic point I want to put across is that these patients should be understood as part of different stages of personality development. It is about time we stopped seeing this condition as "a totally alien process". In trying to understand it as a process in which we all, to different degrees, share, I shall be taking us back to our own adolescence.

Adolescence is a particularly difficult stage when many of us feel inadequate, de-skilled, and misunderstood. Explosive inner feelings and bodily changes occur at such speed that confusion sets in. The outside world appears to be neither tolerant nor patient but actually openly hostile. During this particularly intense and painful phase, we indulge in many fantasies. These serve as a means to fend against an inner experience of a hostile environment.

There are many and varied types of fantasies, from dreams of becoming a famous and intrepid astronaut, to being a dangerous and equally famous gangster. Or, perhaps, a doctor who manages to cure all illnesses of this world, to a bank robber who would be an Oliver Twist and solve all poverty. Or a teacher with much knowledge who is surrounded by adoring children, to a glamorous spy who knows all secrets and displays sexual overtones. Or a nurse who helps everybody, to a prostitute who has special gifts to make people feel better. These dreams have a kaleidoscopic quality in which a complete U-turn happens in seconds. Different polarities overlap and coexist.

Ethics do not count, our survival does.

After a while, this role-playing fades away and is superseded by more realistically oriented achievements. This is all part of a normative process.

However, there are a group of individuals who do not follow this pattern. This normative development is unavailable to them, for many and complicated reasons. Instead, the dreams continue and the acting out goes on. The role-play has become a *modus vivendi*. The "as-if" quality has now acquired a pervasive quality and has become malignant self-deception. This is used as a manic defence against a chronic, masked depression, accompanied by an utter sense of emptiness and nothingness. Some individuals carry out these antisocial actions as regulators of their self-esteem.

Deception and self-deception are the key features of this condition, rarely mentioned in any description of personality disorder. These are deeply interlinked with identity confusion and an inability to see oneself from another's point of view, since the other is oneself. A sense of false-self, accompanied by low self-esteem with an impaired capacity for thinking processes and impulsive action, are present.

I have tried to demonstrate with my clinical examples that at times there are developments in some of these individuals that denote a different dynamic. This tends to appear when they are in their thirties and reveals a strong need for internal change. A feeling of frustration emerges, and some emptiness comes to the fore. The sense of excitement accompanying the acting out is no longer present but has been replaced by plain fear. The actions are now devoid of professionalism, and they feel deskilled. The "mini-kit survival" that has so far been used effectively against the black depression is no longer functioning.

We should be aware of this possibility, since it may indicate a developmental progress and a need for a move from a false-self–centred internal world to one of acknowledgement of a sense of futility and despair. This may lead to integration with others and others' needs.

Its detection is essential and should be equated with a crucial time in the emotional growth of a child–adolescent–young adult in which an input of extra understanding was needed. It requires an open mind to dynamic changes that do not always necessarily include a career of recidivism.

Acting out can easily escalate into a life of law-breaking and crime, and this is when we see such patients and assess their suitability for treatment. The difficulty is that in this field the concept of treatability is frequently equated with curability – which is totally inappropriate. In my own view, forensic psychotherapy is *the* appropriate subspecialty equipped to face this therapeutic challenge.

Indeed, my own failures slowly began to emerge as successes when I was able to allow my patients to become my teachers, and my colleagues my fellow students, in dealing with difficult predicaments involving serious risks to others and themselves.

Many years ago I decided that my work in therapeutic groups should be carried out exclusively with forensic patients within the NHS. I have felt extremely privileged over the years to have been, at times, the container of my patients' "awful" and terrifying predicaments, but at other times a rubbish bag for all their "dirty secrets". And it is this dynamic, continuous countertransferential change, this duality of patient and therapist, the plethora of countertransference feelings, that makes this task unique. If you work hard in therapy to make sense of your experiences, eventually the work will pay off, even if the understanding comes decades later on.